Games, Ideas and Activities for Early Years Literacy

Games, Ideas and Activities for Early Years Literacy

Gill Coulson and Lynn Cousins

Longman
is an imprint of

Harlow, England • London • New York • Boston • San Francisco • Toronto
Sydney • Tokyo • Singapore • Hong Kong • Seoul • Taipei • New Delhi
Cape Town • Madrid • Mexico City • Amsterdam • Munich • Paris • Milan

PEARSON EDUCATION LIMITED
Edinburgh Gate
Harlow CM20 2JE
United Kingdom
Tel: +44 (0)1279 623623
Fax: +44 (0)1279 431059
website: www.pearsoned.co.uk

First edition published in Great Britain in 2011

The right(s) of Gill Coulson and Lynn Cousins to be identified as authors of this work
has been asserted by them in accordance with the Copyright, Designs and Patents Act 1988.

ISBN: 978-1-4082-5417-2

British Library Cataloguing in Publication Data
A CIP catalogue record for this book can be obtained from the British Library

Library of Congress Cataloging in Publication Data
A CIP catalog record for this book can be obtained from the Library of Congress

10 9 8 7 6 5 4 3 2 1
15 14 13 12 11

Cartoon illustrations by Cathy Hughes
Set by 30
Printed in Great Britain by Henry Ling Ltd., at the Dorset Press, Dorchester, Dorset

For Lily
GC

For Mel
LC

Contents

Introduction

Games, Ideas and Activities for Early Years Literacy will provide you with a wealth of resources to enhance your delivery of the Communication, Language and Literacy (CLL) area of learning in the Early Years Foundation Stage (EYFS).

Combining aspects from different areas of learning is recognised as good early years practice. Making connections helps children to make sense of their world and their learning and offers opportunities to reinforce their skills. So, although we have organised these literacy activities into three discrete areas, there will obviously be elements of all aspects of literacy in any activity. Whenever children are writing, for example, they also need to read what they have written, and whenever one child is speaking someone else will be listening. The interdependence of literacy skills will always exist. We have chosen one area of literacy to have greater weight for each activity, but you may decide to modify the activity and focus on a different aspect of literacy.

The three parts of this book are in line with the main elements of the CLL area of learning: talking, reading and writing. Each of these is then sub-divided into three sections, as follows:

Talking

Includes: *Language for Communication* and *Language for Thinking*.

- **Sharing ideas:** encouraging children to contribute to conversations and discussions as they listen to others, take turns and respect other people's ideas.
- **Saying what I mean:** helping children to become more precise in their language, in the way they express their thoughts and ideas, and by developing their working vocabulary.
- **Remember, reflect, retell:** helping children to remember details and sequence events, as they listen well, think about what they have heard, and recall key elements.

Reading

Covers: *Reading*.

250+ activities for *Linking Sounds and Letters* can be found in our other book in the Classroom Gems series – *Early Years Phonics*.

- **World of books:** introducing children to how books work, and ideas to help you use your book area in imaginative ways to create a stimulating and welcoming environment.
- **Finding out:** introducing children to the print that is all around them in posters and signs, and in non-fiction such as instructions or recipes, as well as learning to recognise some common words.
- **Enjoying stories and rhymes:** helping children to recognise the elements of a good story by sharing published literature in activities based on well-known stories and rhymes.

Writing
Includes *Writing* and *Handwriting*.

- **Finger play:** fun ways to practise fine motor skills ready for handwriting, as well as opportunities to use the basic letter shapes.
- **Writing it down:** activities across all areas of the curriculum which help children learn about the importance of recording information.
- **Making a book:** writing down your ideas – factual or creative – in ordered ways to make books in all shapes and sizes to share.

'Literacy should be at the heart of curriculum planning'
Primary National Strategy, 2006, p. 20.

The activities have all been designed to fit in with things that happen every day in an Early Years setting so that they can easily be included in your curriculum plans. There are ideas for each area of the curriculum, including using your role-play area, exploring the world, creating art and display and learning how to make friends. There is a strong emphasis on practical participation and many activities take the children outside, in line with the recommendations of the Early Years Foundation Stage. There are ideas for creating interesting scenarios for talking and many of the activities provide opportunities for assessment.

In each section there are suggestions for using stories, poems or rhymes as an inspiration for children's own reading, writing and talking. Reading stories aloud to children is of course a valuable experience in itself, not only sharing the pleasure of reading but also modelling the rhythms and structure of language and widening children's vocabulary.

Each activity stands alone so you can do as many or as few as you wish. Although we suggest other curriculum areas that might link to the activity, the ideas are flexible and can often be adapted to fit into other themes in your planning. The activities can easily be pitched to different levels of ability and you will find that many are suitable for small groups and therefore ideal for a support assistant to use with those children who need extra practice or opportunities to extend themselves.

The page layout has clear headings and is user-friendly.

Title: where there are a number of activities on one theme or based on the same book we have numbered these (*1*) so that you can combine the activities if you wish.

A 'paper-clipped' note: underneath the title of each activity we briefly introduce and explain the activity to help you find the one that suits your needs.

Aim: the aim of the activity comes directly from the CLL section of the EYFS. It is based on any of the four categories (Developing matters, Look, listen, note, Effective practice, or Planning and resources) and can therefore be easily used in your planning if required.

Resources: any resources that are needed are listed.

Preparation: if there is anything you need to do beforehand, this is indicated.

What to do: the activity is explained in step-by-step instructions and includes ideas and examples to aid the busy practitioner.

Vocabulary: new or unfamiliar vocabulary developed through the activity is clearly listed.

Tip: A handy tip offers additional helpful advice to ensure the smooth running of the activity or to suggest how an activity might be extended or adapted.

Cross-curricular: this alerts the practitioner to where the activity fits in with another of the six areas of learning in the EYFS, thus making maximum use of your preparation.

Children's learning and competence in communicating, speaking and listening, being read to and beginning to read and write must be supported and extended. They must be provided with opportunity and encouragement to use their skills in a range of situations and for a range of purposes, and be supported in developing the confidence and disposition to do so.

Practice Guidance for the Early Years Foundation Stage, May 2008, p. 41.

Young children learn as they play and it's important that they enjoy what they are doing and see a purpose in their learning. In this book you will find lots of fun activities based on play that will help to develop your children's communication and literacy skills.

About the authors

Gill Coulson and Lynn Cousins have worked extensively in primary schools, mainly teaching in the Early Years and Key Stage One. Gill was a deputy head, and Lynn was head of an infant school with Beacon status.

They have both continued to study throughout their teaching careers; Gill gained an M.Phil. degree, researching the teaching of reading, and Lynn gained an MA(Ed.) in early years education.

Since leaving the school environment, Lynn has been an editor of educational publications and is a freelance writer on education. She has a number of published books and was involved in compiling *The International Primary Curriculum* with Fieldwork Education.

Throughout her career, Gill has maintained a strong interest in children's literature, using it as an inspiration in the classroom, helping children learn to read and compose their own writing. She is currently teaching focused writing groups in a number of Milton Keynes schools.

Gill and Lynn have written *Early Years Phonics* in the Classroom Gems series, and Lynn has written *Shaping Children's Behaviour in the Early Years* for the Essential Guides series.

Acknowledgements

Authors' acknowledgements

With thanks to the authors, poets and artists who have inspired us and many children.

Publisher's acknowledgements

We are grateful to the following for permission to reproduce copyright material:

Extract on page xii from *Practice Guidance for the Early Years Foundation Stage*, May 2008, p. 41 (Department for Children, Schools and Families), © Crown copyright 2008; Epigraph on page 2 from *Primary Framework for Literacy and Mathematics*, p. 17 (Primary National Strategy 2006), © Crown copyright 2006; Epigraphs on pages 108 and 230 from *Practice Guidance for the Early Years Foundation Stage*, May 2008, p. 42 (Department for Children, Schools and Families), © Crown copyright 2008. Crown Copyright material is reproduced with permission under the terms of the Click-Use License.

In some instances we have been unable to trace the owners of copyright material, and we would appreciate any information that would enable us to do so.

Part 1
Talking

Given the significance of speaking and listening for children's learning and overall language development, it is important to . . . identify places in the timetable where children can revisit, apply and extend the speaking and listening skills which they have been explicitly taught.

Primary Framework for Literacy and Mathematics, 2006, p. 17.

As children develop speaking and listening skills they build the foundations for literacy, for making sense of visual and verbal signs and ultimately for reading and writing.

Practice Guidance for the Early Years Foundation Stage, May 2008, p. 41.

Chapter 1
Sharing ideas

Introducing circle time

> Encourage the children to come up with ideas for making Circle Time successful.

Aim

- To help children demonstrate appropriate conventions in a group.

Resources

- A small object such as a shiny, smooth shell or stone, small enough to fit in a child's hand.

Preparation

- Sit together quietly.

What to do

- Explain to the children that you are going to spend some time sharing some ideas together. Everyone should be able to see and hear everyone else. Ask them what they think would be a good way to sit so that everyone can do this. Let children offer their own suggestions.
- When a circle is suggested ask the children to move quietly so that everyone is sitting that way. Can everyone see everyone else? Tell them that when we sit like this we call it 'circle time'.
- Explain that when they are in circle time there have to be some rules so that everyone gets a chance to speak, and to make sure that everyone listens carefully. Encourage the children to suggest some rules.
- As they make their suggestions repeat them in positive ways, e.g. if the child says, 'We mustn't shout', you say, 'We must do what then?' 'We must speak quietly – but clearly, so that everyone can hear.'

- Gather together a few rules about speaking one at a time, listening to each other, being polite about other people and so on.
- Have your small object ready. Show this to the children, and tell them that this would be a way to help them to remember about speaking one at a time. The person who is holding this is the only person who can speak. They must be ready to pass it on when they have had their turn.
- Practise using this small object. You start, saying something like, 'My name is . . .'. Then hand it to the next child in the circle. When it gets back to you say a new starter sentence.
- You are now ready to engage the children in other circle time activities.

Try: **www.circle-time.co.uk** for more ideas.

Collins, M. (2001) *Circle Time for the Very Young*, London: Paul Chapman Publishing.

Vocabulary

listen, take turns, speak clearly, polite

Tip

Some useful starter sentences could be:

I like it when . . . . . .

I am sad when . . . . .

My favourite food is . . . .

My friend . . . . is special because . . . .

Cross-curricular link

PSED: Dispositions and Attitudes.

Garden centre (1)

Plan and make some model plants to sell in your garden centre.

Aim

- To ask children to think about how they will accomplish a task, talking through the sequence of stages.

Resources

- A selection of seedlings/plants at various stages of growth
- Small pots filled with plasticene or dough (soil)
- Green straws, green paper (stems and leaves)
- Coloured paper (flower heads)
- Edible seeds (flower seeds)

Preparation

- Plant and care for seeds over a number of weeks so that the children are aware of the stages of growth.

What to do

- Talk about the pattern of growth of the plants the children have grown. Can they remember the order of the stages, e.g.
  - pot of soil with the seeds hidden inside it
  - a small shoot showing through the soil
  - a seedling with leaves
  - a plant with a bud
  - a plant with a flower
  - a plant with seeds forming
- Explain to the children that they are going to make some models of plants to sell in their shop. Talk about which stage of growth each child would like to make. Will it be a seedling or will it have a bud?

- Show the children all the resources that you have collected together. Identify the resources and ask what each one might be used for.
- Can they tell you what they might use to make their own set of plants? Can they tell you what they will do first?
- Let the children make their own versions of the plants. As they work, ask questions about what they are doing, why they are doing it and what they will do next.

Vocabulary

first, next, later, afterwards, last

Tip If possible, provide some real plants at different stages of growth to remind the children of what happens.

Cross-curricular link

KUW: Exploration and Investigation.

Follow-the-leader

Children organise their own parade, deciding on costumes and instruments, and planning everyone's position.

Aim

- To help children talk about and plan their roles.

Resources

- Dressing-up clothes, including hats, beads, scarves
- Musical instruments, e.g. shakers and tambourines

Preparation

- Practise playing follow-the-leader – without dressing up.
- Make sure all the children know what to do, encouraging them to look at the person leading and copy what they do. Include sound effects as well as different movements.
- Children can take it in turns to be the leader for a short time.

What to do

- Place boxes of clothes, accessories and instruments outside so that children can get dressed up and choose an instrument.
- Decide who will be the leader of your parade, and then the order of those who will follow.
  - Look at how everyone is dressed. Do you want all your princesses together?
  - Children can decide whether to use instruments or not and whether they sing, or whether it will be a very quiet parade.
  - Should the instruments lead the parade?
- Take your parade all over the grounds.
- Leave the resources out, ready for children to use later.

Vocabulary

first, in front, behind, next to

 Tip You may need to restrict the space that can be used by the parade so that other children can play safely with other equipment.

Cross-curricular link

PD: Movement and Space.

At the doctor's

Thinking about the conversations that would be appropriate in a doctor's surgery.

Aim

- To encourage children to take turns, listen to others and use appropriate conventional expressions.

Resources

Role-play area set up as a doctor's surgery

What to do

- Talk with a small group of children about the parts they will play in this session – patient, receptionist, nurse and doctor. Help the children dress up in the appropriate clothes for their part.
- Explain that the patient has hurt their leg and needs to see the doctor. Ask them to think about:
  - how the patient hurt their leg
  - what the doctor will need to ask the patient
  - what the receptionist might say to the patient
  - how the nurse will help the doctor

  Give the children time to plan what they will say and how they will say it.
- The children act out the scenario of a patient coming to the doctor's surgery with an injured leg, e.g.
  - The receptionist greets the patient and asks them to take a seat, then tells the doctor the patient has arrived.
  - The nurse helps the patient walk to the doctor, who asks how the leg was hurt.
  - The patient explains and the doctor examines the leg, asking questions to find out where the pain is.

- The doctor asks the nurse to pass items needed to treat the injury, then tells the patient when they need to see the doctor again.
- Before the patient leaves, the receptionist makes a new appointment.

Vocabulary

please, thank you, Can I. . . .? How did you. . . . ?, Where . . .?

Tip The first time the children do this activity, it may be appropriate for the adult to take one of the parts to model the type of conversation.

Cross-curricular link

CD: Developing Imagination and Imaginative Play.

Emergency! by Margaret Mayo (1)

Enjoy a book that has lots of exciting and interesting descriptive words.

Aim

- To extend children's vocabulary.

Resources

- A copy of Mayo, M. (2003) *Emergency!,* London: Orchard Books
- A selection of emergency vehicles as featured in the book

Preparation

- Read and enjoy the book with the children

What to do

- Sit in a circle with the emergency vehicles in the centre. As you read each page of the book, choose a child to point to the vehicle mentioned on that page. Then everyone can repeat the line *'Help is coming – it's on the way!'* as the child returns to their place in the circle.
- When you have finished the book and all the vehicles have been identified, tell the children that this time you will only read the bit that describes the emergency and they must try to remember which vehicle came to help, e.g. *'Emergency! Traffic build-up on the motorway – who can help?'*
- Choose a child who knows the answer to pick up the vehicle while you read the description of the vehicle moving, e.g.

  *'Vroom! Police motorbike
  zipping, revving, cars directing'*

- The child can then repeat the phrase *'Help is coming – it's on the way!'* before they return to their place in the circle.

- Finally, tell the children that this time you are going to describe what the vehicle is doing and they have to guess which vehicle it is. Read the section of text that describes the sound and movement of the emergency vehicle, e.g.

  'zoom on their way, swoop, swoop, swooping and water scooping'

  Can anyone guess which vehicle it is?
- The child who identifies the vehicle correctly can move the vehicle around the inner circle while you reread the relevant page.
- Leave the toy vehicles out with the play-mat so the children can act out some of these emergency situations in their free play.

Vocabulary

police car, breakdown truck, ambulance, helicopter, snow plough, lifeboat, inflatable boat, police motorbike, fire-fighting plane, fire engine, crane

Tip The children might enjoy acting out some of these emergency situations outside during imaginative play. You could call out the emergency and the children pretend to drive or fly the vehicles that come to the rescue

Cross-curricular link

PSED: Sense of Community.

Wedding (1)

Organise a wedding for your teddies, encouraging children to explain their choices.

Aim

- To help children to expand on what they say.

Resources

- Photos from a wedding
- A selection of teddies and dolls
- Dolls' clothes and other items, e.g. camera, flowers, veil, book

What to do

- Have any of the children been to a wedding? Encourage them to talk about their experiences.
- Look at the photographs and identify the bride, etc. Talk about other people who are involved, e.g. the registrar (or other official), photographer.
- Share experiences until everyone has a simple understanding of what happens.
- Let the children choose which teddies will be married and which will play other parts. Ask them to explain their choices.
- Show them the selection of clothing available. Ask the children to choose what each teddy should wear, encouraging them to negotiate. Let them get the toys ready for the wedding.
- Clear a space where the wedding can be held and act it out.

Vocabulary

bride, groom, bridesmaid, guest, registrar, photographer, dress, jacket, tie, veil, flowers, camera

Tip Be sensitive to different cultural experiences.

Cross-curricular link

PSED: Sense of Community.

Collect and sort

Children have fun matching objects to their possible descriptions.

Aim

- To extend the children's vocabulary by grouping and naming.

Resources

- Large paper plates
- Access to small objects around the room
- Hoops
- Paper for labels

Preparation

- Make a selection of labels, each one with a single descriptive word on it, e.g. shiny, smooth, hard.
- Give each child a paper plate and ask them to collect ten small objects from around the room. They should all fit on the paper plate.

What to do

- When the children have ten objects each, they should sit in a circle with the plate on the floor in front of them.
- Place a hoop in the middle of your circle. Reach into your pile of labels and pick one at random. You may want to ask individual children to reach into a container full of your labels and pick one.
- Place the label in the hoop and tell the children that you are looking for objects that are . . . . ., e.g. shiny.
- Go round the circle asking each child in turn, 'Do you have something shiny to go in the hoop?'

- Each child in turn looks at his own selection of objects and chooses one – or not.
- As the game progresses children may start to wish they had saved their red squashy toy for 'squashy' as they had several red objects they could have chosen for 'red'. But no one knows what the labels will say!
- If you play this again on another day, will children choose a wider selection of materials?

Vocabulary

Any descriptive words, such as: shiny, smooth, hard, soft, round, red (etc.), long, thin, fat, squashy, solid, heavy

Tip Add to your labels if you play this again so that the children can't anticipate the criteria.

Cross-curricular link

PSRN: Calculating.

Bert's day

Make up a story about a character, using everyone's ideas about what should happen throughout his day.

Aim

- To encourage children to make up their own stories.

Resources

- Play-mat
- Model buildings
- Toy van

Preparation

- Lay out your play-mat with a selection of buildings, e.g. garage, shop, farm, houses.
- Take it outside on a fine day.

What to do

- Choose a name for your main character, e.g. Bert. Explain to the children that they are going to help you tell the story of Bert's day.
- Choose a different child who will be Bert driving his van at each stage of the story.
- Tell the children that Bert is off in his van to go to the garage to get some petrol. A child will 'drive' the van along the roads on the play-mat.
- While he is there he sees some bunches of flowers for sale. He buys some for his mum.
- He drives his van to his mum's house. Decide which house is his mum's and which of the roads he will drive along. When he gets there he gives his mum the flowers. She loves them.

- She asks Bert to take a jar of the jam she has been making to Old Tom . . . . . .
- The story continues in this way. Every time Bert delivers something he is asked to go somewhere else with another delivery.
- How will the story end?

Vocabulary

Any repetitive phrase that you can include in the story

Tip   This story structure lends itself to a drama activity as you can create parts for as many children as are in your group.

Cross-curricular link

CD: Developing Imagination and Imaginative Play.

Invisible ink

Sharing ideas on why things happen as the children discover the magic of wax-resist.

Aim

- To encourage children to listen attentively and respond with relevant comments.

Resources

- White paper
- White wax crayons
- Thin, watery paint

Preparation

- Ensure the children have had plenty of experience making marks with crayons.

What to do

- Gather a small group of children around the art table or work outside if it's fine. Tell the children you are going to write a secret message.
- Colour some bold letter shapes with the white crayon on a piece of white paper. Ask the children:

    'Why can't they see the message clearly?'
    'Why isn't white a good colour to use?'

- Explain that it's invisible. Then look disappointed – 'Oh dear, but how will anyone see the message?' Ask if anyone has any suggestions of what to do.
- Show them the paint. Tell them you have an idea of how to see the invisible message.

SHARING IDEAS   23

- Lightly paint over the paper and see how the marks show through the paint.
- Can the children explain why it has happened? Listen to their ideas.
- Let the children have a go at writing an invisible message then painting over it.

Vocabulary

white, invisible, shiny, smooth, resist

Tip The marks need to be quite bold and thick, and the paint needs to be thin enough if this activity is going to work.

Cross-curricular link

KUW: Exploration and Investigation.

Mixing paint (1)

> Encourage the children to predict what they think will happen when they mix colours together.

Aim

- To provide an opportunity for children to present ideas to others.

Resources

- Red, yellow and blue paints
- Paper, brushes and water
- Mixing trays

Preparation

- Plenty of previous opportunities for free painting.

What to do

- Working with a small group of children, talk about the three primary colours.
  - Can they name them?
  - Which do they like best and why?
- Tell the children that they are going to use these to make some new colours.
- Ask them to choose two colours each, e.g. blue and yellow.
- Can they guess what colour they'll make if they mix these two together?
- Let them experiment with mixing two colours together to make a new colour, e.g.
  - red and blue to make purple
  - blue and yellow to make green
  - red and yellow to make orange

- Talk about the new colours they have made, and how they made them. What colours did they start with, and what have they made?
- Now ask them to explain how they made their new colour to another child from the class.

Vocabulary

red, blue, yellow, green, orange, purple, mix

Tip Encourage the children to paint blobs of the colours they use and the colour they make – these can be used to create a display that records their findings.

Cross-curricular link

CD: Exploring Media and Materials.

Mixing paint (2)

> A chance for children to describe what happens when they experiment with colours.

Aim

To provide the children with meaningful speaking and listening activities.

Resources

- Red, blue, black and white paints
- Mixing trays, brushes and paper

Preparation

- You will need to do the painting the day before the sorting activity.

What to do

- Working with a small group of children, tell them that they are going to change the blue and red colours.
- Let each child choose a colour and put some of it on their mixing tray. They then paint a blob of this colour on their paper.
- Now let them add a small amount of black to the colour in their mixing try and paint another blob. Encourage them to compare the darker shade to the original colour and describe what has happened.
- Ask them to predict what will happen when more black is added. Let the children add more black and produce darker shades of their chosen colour.
- Working with another group, repeat the activity, but this time ask the children what they think will happen if they add white to their chosen colour.
- Encourage them to paint blobs by adding white and recording the lighter shades.

- Set the shades of colour aside to dry overnight.
- **Next day:** cut out the blobs of colour so you can make several sets of six shades. Provide time for the children who painted them to explain how they were made.
- Now give out a set of six shades to a pair of children. Ask them to put the colours in order from light to dark. Encourage them to talk and negotiate as they arrange the colours in order.

Vocabulary

red, blue, black, white, mix, dark, darker, light, lighter, paler, paler, shade

Tip Set up a display to remind the children what they have experienced using the blobs of colour, enlarged vocabulary and photographs taken as the children work.

Cross-curricular link

CD: Exploring Media and Materials.

Mini·beasts (1)

> Set up a role-play area that helps children to imagine life from someone else's perspective.

Aim

To encourage children to imagine and recreate roles.

Resources

- Oversized T-shirts in a variety of plain colours

Preparation

- Set up a role-play area as a garden:
  - Make oversized paper leaves, grass and flowers from paper. Fix these to a wall display board at ground level. It should resemble a giant garden. Do this as a separate activity with the children.
- Put the T-shirts in a crate or basket nearby.

What to do

- Gather the children together near the 'garden' they have made. All sit on the floor so that the 'grass' etc is taller than them.
- Talk about the height of the 'grass' etc. compared to their height.

    'This is what a garden must look like to a spider or a beetle'.

- Ask the children to imagine being an insect in the garden. Can they think of anything else that might be in a garden and that would look big to a spider, but not to us, e.g.
  - a foot
  - a ball
  - a bird

- Encourage the children to play in the garden they have made wearing one of the T-shirts to look like the mini-beast that they want to be. You could try black for a beetle, red for a ladybird, etc.

Vocabulary

huge, tiny

Tip

Write out some nursery rhymes about mini-beasts. Put them near your 'garden' and read them together. Try:

Little Miss Muffet

Incy Wincy Spider

Ladybird, Ladybird, Fly Away Home

Cross-curricular link

CD: Developing Imagination and Imaginative Play.

Rhyming instructions

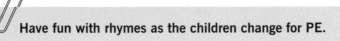

Have fun with rhymes as the children change for PE.

Aim

- To encourage children to enjoy using rhyming words.

Resources

- PE kits
- Adult helpers

Preparation

- Make up a simple rhyme to fit your circumstances (see example below).

What to do

- Let the children collect their bags that contain their PE clothes, ready to get changed for PE.
- Tell the children you have made up a special little rhyme to remind them what to do. Ask them to listen out for the rhyming words as you say it.
  Can anyone guess the ending?

  Put your bag on the table
  Put your clothes on the chair
  Put your shoes on the floor
  And put your socks in there!

- Keep repeating the rhyme as they get ready for PE. Encourage the children to join in. Will anyone remember it next time?
- Can the children help make up rhymes for other routines, e.g., juice time/lunch time/getting ready for going home?

Vocabulary

Pairs of rhyming words: chair – there, last – fast, ready – steady, stop – hop.

 Tip More ideas for working with rhythm and rhyme can be found in *Games, Ideas and Activities for Early Years Phonics* in the Classroom Gems series.

Cross·curricular link

PSED: Self-care.

Should we paint today?

Children create different weather conditions and talk about how they affect their painting.

Aim

- To help children to link cause and effect to explain their choices.

Resources

- Paint, paper and easels
- Straws, watering can, newspaper
- Aprons and waterproof covering

Preparation

- Set up four painting easels outside on a fine day with no wind. This is a messy activity so position it away from walls, other activities or the door into the setting.

What to do

- Explain to the children that they are going to think about painting outdoors. Sometimes we can do this, sometimes we can't.
- One reason for this might be the weather. Why? Listen to the children's ideas and talk about them.

    'What difference would it make if it was breezy, or very windy?'
    'What if it was showery or there was a heavy rainstorm?'

- Tell the children that they are going to make these four different kinds of weather today so that they can find out what would happen to their paintings in these different conditions. Encourage the children to suggest some ideas for creating weather effects, eg:

Activity 1: A breezy day
Paint your picture. While it is wet,
– blow onto it
– blow through a straw onto it

Activity 2: A very windy day
Paint your picture. While it is wet,
– flap a newspaper near it
– take it off the easel and wave it around

Activity 3: A showery day
Paint your picture. While it is wet,
– splash water onto it with your fingers
– use a pipette to drip water all over it

Activity 4: A wet day
– wet the paper before you paint your picture
– use a watering can to soak the paper after you have painted your picture.

- Have two children at each of the four activities. Start by asking the children to discuss what they think will happen with 'their' weather.
- Observe them as they carry out the activity. When they have finished, ask them:

  'What happened?'
  'Why?'
  'Were you right?'
  'Would this be a good painting day?'

Vocabulary

reason, effect, decision

 Tip Children can work in pairs at different activities and then come together as a group to report their findings.

Cross-curricular link

KUW: Exploration and Investigation.

What a lot of nonsense!

Make up some silly words as you adapt a well-known rhyme.

Aim

- To encourage children to experiment with words and sounds.

Resources

A copy of 'Fingers Like to Wiggle, Waggle' in Matterson, E. (compiler) (1991), *This Little Puffin,* London: Penguin.

Preparation

- Enjoy singing this finger rhyme with the children.

What to do

- Ask the children to show you how to wiggle their fingers as they join in the rhyme.
- Tell them the next time you say the rhyme you are going to try something new.
- Start to tap your fingers together as you begin the rhyme.
- Ask the children to suggest words for this movement, e.g.

  tippy tappy

Sing the first verse.
- Tell the children they can say any silly words they like as they move their fingers.
- Ask for ideas, e.g.

  bingy bongy
  dimby dumby

  Enjoy the frivolity as their words get sillier and sillier!

- Choose a few favourites that work well. Then tell the children which ones to use for each of the four verses. Encourage them to keep moving their fingers as they say their silly words.

Vocabulary

Any two-syllable nonsense words that begin with the same initial sound

Tip You might want to use this activity to focus on alliteration by choosing two words that start with the same sound, or on rhythm by demonstrating the two syllables in *wiggle* and *waggle* by clapping.

Cross-curricular link

CD: Creating Music and Dance.

Asking questions

Plan a set of questions that the children could ask a visitor.

Aim

- To help the children to form questions appropriate for a visitor.

Resources

- Question words prepared on card or interactive whiteboard, e.g. what, when, where, how, who.

Preparation

- Arrange a visitor who will come to talk to the children about their job, e.g. librarian, nurse or policeman.

What to do

- Tell the children that you are going to have a visitor and who it is. Ask them what they know about this person's work.
- Tell the children that you want to get some questions ready to ask the visitor.
  - What would they like to find out?
- Show the children the question words. Read each word in turn.
- Model how to create a question with one of the words, for your visitor, e.g.
    'What part of your job do you enjoy best?'
    'Where do you go to work?'
    'Who do you work with?'
- Try to form questions like these which are open-ended and allow the visitor to talk rather than just answer yes or no.

- Help the children think of more questions to ask, e.g.

    'When did you decide to be a nurse?'
    'How do you arrest people?'

- Write down their ideas and let them practise asking them.

Vocabulary

what, when, where, how, who

Tip Keep a copy of the children's questions to prompt them when the visitor is there.

Cross-curricular link

PSED: Sense of Community.

Problem-solving (1)

How will the children cooperate with each other as they try to sort themselves out in height order?

Aim

- To encourage children to work with others to devise a plan.

Preparation

- This will follow on from some work on comparing sizes.

What to do

- Explain to the children that you want them to stand in a line with the tallest child at one end, and the smallest child at the other end.
- To do this they will need to find out who is the tallest in the whole group, who is the second tallest and so on. They should work together to sort out the answer.
- Let them try for a little while. Observe them to see how they are working it out.
  - Is any one child organising the group?
  - Are they allowing everyone else to contribute ideas?
- Stop the group and gather them all together.
  - Ask them to tell you how they are trying to work this out.
  - Give everyone time to add their own ideas or comment on suggestions put forward by others.
- Ask the children to complete the activity. Remind children to ask, e.g.

  'May I . . .?'
  'Should we . . .?'
  'What do you think about . . .?'

Vocabulary

taller, shorter

Tip If your group is quite small or struggling with the activity, suggest they compare any two children and then take the taller one each time and compare that child with another. Continue until you have the tallest person. Repeat for each position in turn.

Cross·curricular link

PSRN: Shape, Space and Measures.

Problem-solving (2)

A chance for children to cooperate and negotiate as they build a shelter from the sun.

Aim

- To work with other children to negotiate plans and activities.

Resources

- Large piece of fabric
- String

Preparation

- Look around your outside area.
- Where would you fix a shelter?
- Are there any trees, railings, etc. which may be useful?
- If not, leave some chairs, boxes, lengths of wood, etc. outside.

What to do

- Explain to the children that they have been shipwrecked. Decide how far your 'island' extends within your grounds. They have to stay on this 'island' until a boat comes to pick them up, so they need to build a shelter to keep the hot sun off them.
- Provide a small group of children with a piece of fabric and the string. This is all that was washed up from their ship!
- Explain that they have to work together to find a place to build their shelter, and a method for doing it. Provide help with tying knots in the string etc., but encourage the children to come up with their own solution to the problem.

- Take note of the group dynamics:
  - Who takes the lead?
  - Who is content to leave it to others?
  - Who works hard in the team?

Vocabulary

shelter, protect, safe

Tip Make these on hot days and use them as real shelters.

Cross-curricular link

PSED: Self-care.

Problem-solving (3)

> Working together, the children help Teddy find a way to retrieve the doll's shoe from the water tray.

Aim

- To encourage children to interact with others, creating and testing plans.

Resources

- Water tray
- Teddy
- Doll
- Doll's shoe

Preparation

- Before the children arrive, put the doll's shoe in the centre of the water tray.

What to do

- Tell the children that whilst they were at home last night, Teddy was messing about. He threw the doll's shoe into the water tray and then couldn't reach it to get it back out. The doll is very upset about it.
- Ask them if they can work out a way for Teddy to get the shoe out. Make sure that they understand that Teddy has to do this – they can't simply reach in and get it for him.
- Spend time talking about their ideas. They may decide on, e.g.
  - Something that is long that Teddy can reach with and hook the shoe out (perhaps a fishing net, or a stick with something tied to the end of it).
  - Something that will float on the water and will carry Teddy across to get the shoe out with his paws (a boat, a piece of wood or anything else that they can find to float).

- Encourage children to think through their ideas, talking about 'if' and 'could', before they actually test their idea.
- At the end of the session each group of children in turn can explain their plan to the others. Did it work?

Vocabulary

Useful questions to encourage discussion: What would happen if . . . . .? Is it possible that . . . .? Could we . . . . .? Is it safe to . . . . . .?

 Tip   This is a good opportunity to reinforce water safety rules.

Cross-curricular link

KUW: Exploration and Investigation.

Chapter 2
Saying what I mean

Café (1)

Discuss what will be needed to set up a café. Encourage the children to think carefully about the equipment and organisation as an adult records their ideas.

Aim

- To provide activities where children use talk to anticipate what they will be doing.

Resources

- Large piece of paper and pens for adult to scribe ideas

Preparation

Encourage children to share their experiences of going to cafes. Some questions to ask them are:
- What do you like to eat and drink?
- Who do you go with?
- Do you know the café's name or where it is?
- Have you been to a café for a special occasion?
- Have you sat outside at a café?

What to do

- Tell the children you are going to create a café. Ask them to think what will be needed.
  Draw pictures or write simple words to record the children's suggestions, e.g., plates, cutlery, cups, tables and chairs.
- To guide their planning ask them to think about:
  - How will the customers pay?
  - How will they know what they can choose?
  - How do they place an order?

The children might decide they need to have a food counter and pay at a till, or they might want waiters and waitresses.
- It will be quite easy to change the café from one style to another to give more variety after a few days. During the summer months you could try setting up the café outside or try creating an ice cream van!

Vocabulary

cake, sandwich, burger, coke, juice, fruit, ice cream, menu, till, customer, waiter/ress

 Tip Try changing your café to offer different types of food, e.g. Indian, Chinese or Caribbean.

Cross-curricular link

CD: Developing Imagination and Imaginative Play.

Hunt the book

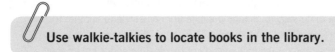

Use walkie-talkies to locate books in the library.

Aim

- To encourage children to use talk to organise and clarify thinking.

Resources

- Simple walkie-talkie device
- Access to a library or book collection outside of the classroom or working area

Preparation

- Check the books available so that you know what is there at the time of this activity.

What to do

- Explain to the children that two of them are going to go to the library and choose a book.
  They will need to remember what it looks like and where it is, then they return to the classroom.
- Two other children now go to the library with the walkie-talkie.
- The two children in the classroom guide the two in the library to find the same book.
- Think about:
  - Is it on the top shelf?
  - Is it a big book?
  - What is the picture on the cover?
  - What colour is it?

- The two in the classroom keep giving clues until the others think they have found it.
  They return, with the book, to find out whether they have located the right book.
- Now swap roles.

 Tip If you have two copies of any book, use one in each area for less able or younger children.

Cross-curricular link

KUW: ICT.

Wolf!

The children listen carefully to instructions as they play a musical Red Riding Hood game.

Aim

- To help children to listen and respond with relevant actions.

Resources

- Music to dance to

Preparation

- You will need a large space to play in.
- Set up your music.

What to do

- Choose a few children to be trees, to make the forest. If you have extra adults, they could play this role. The 'trees' should spread their arms out like branches.
- Everyone else dances round the trees to the music.
- When the music stops, call out an instruction. The children can choose how they act out the instruction. Try:
  - Pick some flowers for Grandma
  - Skip down the path
  - Check the cakes in your basket
  - Your hood has come off
  - Eat one of the cakes
- But sometimes you will call out WOLF!! Then everyone must quickly hide behind a tree. The last person to hide is 'out' and becomes another tree, until there is only one person left dancing.

Tip Watch for children who can think of an action quickly. Is there anyone who struggles with this?

Cross-curricular link

CD: Developing Imagination and Imaginative Play.

I do, you do

Children work in pairs to make identical models. One child explains and the other follows the instructions.

Aim

- To provide an opportunity for children to explain instructions clearly, using a range of positional language.

Resources

- Interlocking cubes or coloured bricks
- Something to create a screen across the middle of the table

Preparation

- Two children each have ten cubes or bricks. They should each have an identical mix of colours.
- Seat the children so that they can't see what the other one is doing. They could be back to back, or you could create some sort of screen between them.

What to do

- Child One makes a simple model using any number of their cubes. This could even be a simple line of cubes.
- Child Two has to make an identical model by following instructions.
- Child One gives instructions one at a time, and Child Two signals when they are ready to hear the next instruction.
- When Child Two has finished, the children show each other their models. Are they the same?

Vocabulary

next, after that, on top of, underneath, in between, together

 Tip You may need to demonstrate first, letting both children follow your instructions.

Cross-curricular link

PSRN: Shape, Space and Measures.

Shine a light

Children use a torch and describe exactly what they can see.

Aim

To provide an opportunity for children to use meaningful speaking and listening.

Resources

- One or two small torches
- A dark corner, cupboard or box
- A selection of small toys

Preparation

- Set up your dark area and hide a few toys in there.
- Show the children how to turn the torches on and off.

What to do

- Tell the children that some toys are hidden away in the dark cupboard/box. Explain that everyone will take turns to use the torch to see the toys.
- When they are shining the torch they must choose one toy to describe to the others, e.g.

    'I can see something that is round and smooth and small.'

    Can the other children guess what it is?
- If they guess it correctly, the toy is brought out of the cupboard. Then another child has their turn.

Vocabulary

big, small, soft, hard, shiny, fluffy, round, square, long, thin…

Tip Younger children may need to see the toys and talk about them before they are hidden.

Cross-curricular link

KUW: ICT.

Toot Toot Beep Beep by Emma Garcia (1)

> Help the children to sort the vocabulary in the book into two sets of 'fast' or 'slow' words.

Aim

- To increase the range of children's vocabulary.

Resources

- A copy of Garcia, E. (2009) *Toot Toot Beep Beep,* St Albans: Boxer Books
- Pieces of paper
- Cars
- Two setting circles labeled 'fast' and 'slow'

Preparation

- Remind the children of the story by reading it again.

What to do

- Sit in a circle with the labelled setting circles in the middle.
- Look at the first vehicle in the book. How does it move away?

    'It zooms'.

- Choose a child to take one of the cars and show what 'zoom' would look like.
- Ask the children whether 'zoom' means fast or slow? Once everyone has agreed, write the word 'zoom' on a piece of paper and place it in the correct setting circle.
- Continue through the book, finding the word, testing it out and deciding whether it is going to join 'zoom' as a 'fast' word or it will go into the other circle of 'slow' words.
- When you have a full set of words, read through all the 'fast' words and then all the 'slow' words together.

- Everyone can now take a car. You will read one of the words at a time and they will demonstrate with their car each time – will it be fast or slow?
- Finish with all the cars parking quietly in the car park.

Vocabulary

zoom, speed, trundle, rush, glide, roll, hurtle

Tip   Use this as part of your garage role-play activities.

Cross-curricular link

CLL: Role play.

Telephone your order

Talking on a telephone is a fun way to use adjectives as the children identify or describe a fruit or vegetable.

Aim

- To provide an opportunity for children to participate in meaningful speaking and listening activities.

Resources

- Two toy telephones or out-of-use adult ones
- A selection of fruit and vegetables familiar to the children

Preparation

- Ensure that most children can name the items and describe some of their properties.

What to do

- Sit in a circle with a selection of fruit and vegetables in the centre.
- Explain that you are the customer ringing the greengrocer's shop, but you don't know the names of all the things in the shop. A child will be the shopkeeper who answers the phone and tries to help.

> *Adult: Do you have any vegetables that are hard and long and coloured orange?*
> *Shopkeeper: Yes, we do – they are carrots. How many do you want?*
> *Adult: I would like two large ones please.*
> *Shopkeeper: OK, I'll save two large carrots for you.*
> *Adult: Thank you very much. Goodbye.*

- Let another child take the role of shopkeeper and answer your next call.
- When the children are confident about the game encourage them to play both roles – the customer and the shopkeeper.

Vocabulary

round, long, soft, hard, smooth, big, small, yellow, green, red, orange, purple...

Tip You could play a similar game with zoo or farm animals pretending the customer is setting up a new zoo or farm.

Cross-curricular link

KUW: ICT.

Put it on

> A lively activity helping children to give clear and precise instructions about getting dressed.

Aim

- To encourage children to use talk to organise and sequence events.

Resources

- A large jumper
- If possible, have another adult to be your model

What to do

- Place the jumper on the floor or on a nearby table.
- The children have to tell the adult how to put the jumper on.
  Explain to the children that the adult will do exactly as they suggest.
- Ask the children: 'What should she do first?'
  Children's suggestions may be to 'put your head through the hole'
  The adult should do this – don't pick it up, just try to do it where the jumper is!
  Play it up – make it a comic act.
- Have great fun together as the children try to think of all the stages they have missed out.
- Some children may like to come out and have a go at putting the jumper on.
  Will the others remember all the necessary stages of instructions?

Vocabulary

through, under, inside, outside, over, pull

Tip This could be done on another occasion with shoes that fasten or a coat that needs to be fastened up for a wintry day.

Cross-curricular link

PSED: Self-care.

Is it you?

Children identify someone in the group by responding to your clues.

Aim

- To provide an opportunity for children to use a broad range of adjectives correctly.

Resources

- A set of names of the children in the group, written on individual pieces of paper

What to do

- The game starts with everyone standing up.
- Pick a name at random from those you've written out. Don't let anyone else know who it is.
- Tell the children that they have to work out who it is, e.g.

    'The person I'm thinking of has long hair'
    'So, all those without long hair sit down.'

    'The person I'm thinking of has black shoes'
    'So, all those without black shoes sit down.'

- Continue until there is only one person left standing. Check the name on the piece of paper. Have you found the right child?
- That child then comes to the front and starts the game again by choosing another name.

Vocabulary

long, short, colour words, tall, curly, straight

Tip You may have to help the children work out whether to sit or stay standing until they become more familiar with the game.

Cross-curricular link

PSED: Sense of Community.

Mini·beasts (2)

Children think of words to describe how mini-beasts move before pretending to be one.

Aim

- To extend the children's vocabulary.

Resources

- Drum
- Tambourine or shaker

What to do

- Explain to the children that they are going to pretend to be some of the mini-beasts that live in the garden. Ask everybody to try to move like a butterfly. Then encourage the children to try being a spider. Continue with any other mini-beasts, e.g. a caterpillar, a bee or a snail.
- Sit together and ask them to suggest some words to describe how the different creatures move. Take one mini-beast at a time and collect some words, e.g.

    caterpillars – crawl, creep
    butterflies – float, fly, flap
    spiders – scurry, scamper
    bees – buzz, hover
    beetles – scuttle

  Be ready to add some words so that children can increase their word knowledge.
- Now everyone stands in a space ready to play a game.
- Tell the children that they are to be intrepid explorers, hunting for creatures in the garden. *Move quietly, don't alert them!*

- You beat the drum as the children move stealthily around the space in time to the beat.
- You stop beating the drum, and begin to shake the tambourine or shakers. At the same time call out one of the movements you all thought of:
  - Float like a butterfly
  - Scamper like a spider
  - Hover like a bee, etc

  The children have to follow the instruction, before you start beating the drum again.

Vocabulary

float, fly, flap, scamper, scurry, buzz, hover, scuttle, crawl, creep

Tip Play this outside if you can.

Cross-curricular link

PD: Movement and Space.

Do the digger dance

The children follow your instructions to work in pairs as driver and crane.

Aim

- To encourage children to use talk to give and follow instructions.

Preparation

- Look at cranes in real life if you can.
- Watch a video clip of cranes in action.

What to do

- Ask the children to find a space of their own big enough for them to stretch their arms out in all directions without touching anything, or anyone else.
- Children can practise moving like a crane, e.g.

    'Stretch out your arms and then clasp your hands together to look like the arm of a digger or crane.'

    'Keep your feet still, and move your 'crane' as far as you can.'

    'Now practise shuffling your feet round as you move your 'crane' – but don't move away from your space.'

- Once they can act the part of the crane, give the children verbal instructions as if you were the driver:

    Move your crane up high.
    Turn your crane towards the door.
    Bend your crane down to the ground.
    Wait while someone fastens the big crate onto your hook.
    Now slowly lift your crane. Don't drop the crate.
    Turn towards . . . etc.

- Children can now work in pairs taking it in turn to be the crane or the driver, giving and following instructions.

Vocabulary

up, down, round, towards left, right

Tip   Children could wear a 'hard hat' when they are the driver.

Cross-curricular link

CD: Developing Imagination and Imaginative Play.

What's inside?

Children can investigate and photograph fruit to create a lift-the-flap book or display.

Aim

- To encourage children to use talk to organise and clarify their thinking.

Resources

- Fruit
- Sharp knife
- Camera
- Folded pieces of card and glue

Preparation

- Take some photographs of the fruit you have collected, one photograph for each piece of fruit.

What to do

- Encourage the children to look at the fruit and handle it carefully. Ask them to look, touch and smell as they investigate.
- Try to expand their vocabulary as they compare and describe the fruit, e.g.
  - Which is the heaviest/shiniest/hardest?
  - Has anyone eaten any of these fruits?
  - Can the children explain how it tastes?
- Tell the children you are going to cut the fruit in half. Ask them what they expect to find when the fruit is cut open, e.g. colour, juice or size of stone. Make sure everyone has a chance to explain their ideas.

- When the children are ready, cut the pieces of fruit in half. Let the children describe what they see, smell and feel.
  - Is it what you expected?
- Help the children take photographs of the inside of the fruit. When these are printed out, match them up with the photographs of the outside of the fruit. Stick the photograph of the outside of the fruit on the front of a folded piece of card, and the photograph of the inside of the fruit can be stuck inside the fold.
- The folded cards can either be displayed on the wall to create an interactive display or stuck into a book to create a lift-the-flap book that the children will enjoy reading afterwards.

Vocabulary

hard, soft, smooth, furry, heavy, light, juice, flesh, skin, stone

 Tip If you label the fruit this will help with the children's understanding of how print works.

Cross-curricular link

KUW: Exploration and Investigation.

How are you feeling?

Extend the children's vocabulary and understanding by reading the expression in different faces.

Aim

- To introduce new words into children's vocabulary.

Resources

- Pictures of people with various expressions
- Mirrors

What to do

- Explain that you are going to think about people's faces. Ask them what we see when we look at someone's face and listen to the children's answers.
- Explain that what we are feeling shows on our faces and this is called our expression.
- Illustrate by making a happy face and a sad face. Then encourage the children to use these expressions too.
- Show the children one of your pictures and encourage the children to explain how that person might be feeling, e.g.
  - The person might be looking shocked.
  - Can the children make any suggestions about why this person might be shocked?
  - Have they ever felt shocked?
  - Ask them to show you a shocked expression.
  - Suggest that it helps to think about something that makes you feel that way.
  Repeat the procedure with a different expression.

- Lay all the pictures out on the floor and hand out the mirrors.
- Let each child choose a picture and use the mirror to recreate that expression.
  Take it in turns to show each other their different expressions and talk about how the person in the picture is feeling and why.

Vocabulary

impatient, irritated, shocked, surprised, proud, smug, joyful, tired, worried, lonely, puzzled, angry, pleased, delighted, frightened

 Tip To extend this activity you could try linking two similar expressions and exploring the differences with the children, e.g. shocked and surprised.

Cross-curricular link

PSED: Self-confidence and Self-esteem.

Emergency! by Margaret Mayo (2)

Children describe the various emergencies and who will come and help.

Aim

- To use stories from books to focus children's attention on predictions and explanations.

Resources

- A copy of Mayo, M. (2003) *Emergency!,* London: Orchard Books

Preparation

- Read and enjoy the book with the children.

What to do

- Use the illustrations in the book to ask the children to describe each emergency.
  - Can they explain what has happened?
  - Can they suggest which emergency service will be needed?
  - Can they predict how the emergency service will help?
- The children might also talk about who has phoned for the emergency service, e.g.
  - Was it the man in the sinking boat or the lady on the beach with the umbrella?
- Use a toy telephone to let the children take turns to dial 999 and ask for the service required in the different scenarios shown in the book.

- Use the pictures of the emergency vehicles on the first and last pages of the book.
  - Can the children name each vehicle?
  - Do they know who drives each type of vehicle?
  - Can they remember which emergency each vehicle attended?

Vocabulary

police car, breakdown truck, ambulance, helicopter, snow plough, lifeboat, inflatable boat, police motorbike, fire-fighting plane, fire engine, crane

Tip Be aware that this may be a sensitive topic if children have been involved in emergency situations.

Cross-curricular link

PSED: Sense of Community.

Chapter 3
Remember, reflect, retell

After the big parade

> Work with the children to create a display about a parade that they have seen.

Aim

- To remind the children of a parade by creating a display about it.

Resources

- Souvenirs and photographs of the parade
- Any video clips of a parade in your area
- Back your display board with paper or fabric and add a large label

Preparation

- Many festivals and ceremonies include a parade or procession. You may have a parade as part of your local school or village traditions. Perhaps you have even taken part.

What to do

- Show the video, share out the souvenirs and encourage the children to comment on them.
- Pose the following questions and give time for the children to think about their answers and join in the discussion.
  - What did you see?
  - What did you hear?
  - How did it make you feel?
- Allow time for the children to make paintings or collages of the performers in the parade.
  Cut out the paintings of people in the parade and fix them to the display board, pointing out that people are one behind the other in a parade. Work from left to right, to reinforce the convention of writing.
- Add any other items you have collected to your display.

Vocabulary

first, in front, behind, next to

Tip   Compare one parade with another if children have seen different ones.

Cross-curricular link

PSED: Sense of Community.

Once upon a time (1)

Children make some fairy-story puppets to retell their favourite stories.

Aim

- To use puppets to encourage children to retell stories.

Resources

- Wooden spoons
- Scraps of fabric and elastic bands
- Felt-tip pens and wool

Preparation

- Read the fairy tale that you want to focus on and identify the characters.
- Make your puppets of these characters:

    Use felt-pen to draw a face onto the bowl of the spoon.
    Add some wool 'hair'.
    Use elastic bands to hold some fabric 'clothes' in place over the handle.

What to do

- Read or tell the children the chosen fairy tale again. As you read, the children can act out the story with their puppets.
- Repeat the story. This time the children can add the words/speech of their character, as you pause in the telling of the story.
    - Can they make appropriate voices?
    - What would Grandma sound like?
    - What voice would the wolf use when he was pretending to be Grandma?
    - What voice did Goldilocks use when she was frightened at the end of the story?
- Children can now try to retell the whole story with their puppets.

Tip If different groups of children focus on different stories you can soon collect a range of puppets to leave out for later use. Label some boxes, one for each set of characters.

Cross-curricular link

CLL: Story characters.

Once upon a time (2)

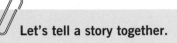

Let's tell a story together.

Aim

- To encourage children to use intonation and story language.

Resources

- A picture book of the story you want to retell (optional – see Tip)

Preparation

- Plenty of opportunities for listening to stories.

What to do

- Sit in a circle together and choose a favourite story that all the children know, e.g. *The Three Little Pigs.* Ask them if they can remember the story.
- Tell them you are going to retell the story together. Ask who would like to start. Prompt them to begin with *'Once upon a time...'*
- When the first child has said a sentence let the next child carry on. Continue around the circle until the end of the story. If a child omits something, be ready to gently prompt them, e.g. 'Oh, don't forget to tell us what he built his house with.' If a child uses incorrect grammar, try to help them rephrase their words, e.g. 'I think you could say: So they both **ran** to the third little pig's house.' If a child struggles to recall the next event in the story, ask if anyone else can help.
- Encourage the children to use repeated phrases from the story, e.g. *'So he huffed and he puffed'*.
- The last child can be prompted to end with *'... and they lived happily ever after'*.

Vocabulary

once upon a time, lived happily ever after, and repeated phrases from the story of your choice

Tip   If the children find this game too difficult at first, use a picture-book version of your story to prompt them.

Cross-curricular link

CLL: Story structure.

Swirling and whirling around

Talking about the magical effects the children can create with oil, washing-up liquid and food colouring.

Aim

- To prompt children's thinking and discussion through involvement in their play.

Resources

- One-litre plastic bottles – one between two children
- Cold water
- Vegetable oil
- Washing-up liquid
- Food colourings
- Pipettes

Preparation

- Make sure the children know how to use pipettes. Have some available for water play in the days before you want to do this activity.

What to do

- Half-fill a bottle with cold water. Drop some food colouring in – one or two drops only. Watch and talk about what you see.
- **EITHER:** Add some washing-up liquid – one or two drops. Watch and talk.
- **OR** Add some cooking oil – one or two drops. Watch and talk.
- Children can experiment with what they add, and the order in which they add things to the water. Be ready with your questions so that you can support their thinking.

Vocabulary

Useful questions include:
>   What are you doing?
>   What will you do next?
>   What do you think will happen?
>   What did you notice?
>   Is this the same as when you added . . . . . first?
>   Do you know why this happened?
>   What happens if you add more than one colour?

 Tip Demonstrate one variation only so that the children are free to use their own ideas for experimenting with the materials.

Cross-curricular link

KUW: Exploration and Investigation.

Birthday (1)

Helping children think about a story and what happens, before acting it out for themselves.

Aim

- To encourage children to respond to and retell stories.

Resources

- Hughes S. (1985) *Alfie Gives a Hand,* London: Collins Picture Lions.

Preparation

- Read the story to the children.
- Discuss with the children:
  - Why Alfie takes his comfort blanket to the party.
  - How Bernard behaves at the party.
- Keep asking the children:
  - What happens next in the story?
  - How does s/he feel?

What to do

- Let the children choose who will be Alfie, Bernard, Min and others at the party. The adult can be Bernard's mother.
- Act out the birthday party.
  - Alfie arrives with his blanket and gives his present to Bernard.
  - All the children play with bubbles, then Bernard pops Min's bubble and she cries.
  - They sit down to tea and sing to Bernard.
  - Bernard frightens Min.
  - Alfie is holding Bernard's hand but Min won't join the circle.
  - Alfie puts down his blanket so he can hold Min's hand too.
  - Everyone plays Ring-a-ring-o'-roses.
- Change roles and try acting out the party scene again.

Vocabulary

worried, sad, shocked, frightened, kind, happy

Tip How does Alfie give a hand? Do the children understand this also means to help?

Cross-curricular link

PSED: Self-confidence and Self-esteem.

Birthday (2)

> Start with a well-known story and have fun suggesting different outcomes.

Aim

To encourage children to predict possible endings to stories and events.

Resources

Hughes, S. (1985) *Alfie Gives a Hand,* London: Collins Picture Lions.

Preparation

- Read the story to the children and discuss Alfie, Min and Bernard's feelings and behaviour.

What to do

- Ask the children what might change if something different happened.
  - What if . . . Alfie had been too worried to go to the party?
  - What if . . . Min had not been scared of Bernard?
  - What if . . . Bernard had been sent to his room to calm down?
  How would the birthday party have turned out then?
- Choose one of the ideas to try. Let the children choose who will be Alfie, Bernard, Min and others at the party. The adult can be Bernard's mother.
- Act out the different birthday party and afterwards compare the outcome with the original story.

Vocabulary

worried, sad, shocked, frightened, kind, happy, sorry, mean, friendly, angry

Tip This would make a good follow-on activity from Birthday (1), p. 84.

Cross-curricular link

PSED: Self-confidence and Self-esteem.

Roses are red

Model how to change the words of a traditional rhyme to send positive messages to each other.

Aim

- To help children make up their own rhyme.

Resources

- Make an enlarged copy of the traditional rhyme

    Roses are red
    Violets are blue
    Sugar is sweet
    And so are you

Preparation

- Teach the children the traditional rhyme.
- If possible, show them roses and violets.

What to do

- Sit in a class circle, and read the traditional rhyme to the children. Let the children follow the words on the enlarged copy.
- Tell the children you are going to change one line of the rhyme to make a new one.
  Explain that you are going to use names from children in the class, and that you are going to use the rhyme to say kind things to each other.
- Demonstrate by choosing one child's name to include in the third line of the rhyme.
  Include another child by pointing at them as you say the last line, e.g.

    Roses are red
    Violets are blue
    James is happy
    And so are you

- Encourage the children to repeat the rhyme with you so that everyone points to any other child when they say the last line.
- Think of other kind things to say about each other. Use these ideas in the rhyme and let everyone repeat them.

Vocabulary

happy, friendly, helpful, kind, cheerful, smart, clever

Tip With more able children you could write down their ideas for them to select and use in their own rhymes.

Cross-curricular link

PSED: Making Relationships.

Take three

Children make up a story together based on three random objects they select.

Aim

- To help children use language to imagine roles and experiences.

Resources

- Small world toys, e.g. farm or zoo animals, vehicles, dolls' house furniture and people.
- Box or basket.

Preparation

- Collect together about ten objects and place them in an attractive box or basket.

What to do

- Sit in a circle with a small group of children.
- Choose one child to close their eyes and reach into the basket. Ask them to choose one object and then open their eyes and tell everyone what it is.
  Repeat this with two other children.
  Place your three objects in the middle of your circle.
- Another child can then choose the setting for your story. It could be e.g.

    the seaside
    the cupboard under the stairs
    a strange planet

- Encourage imaginative ideas.

- Explain to the children that you are all going to help to make up a story involving the three chosen objects and the special place you have decided on.
- Remind the children of familiar story openings, e.g.

  One day ...
  Once upon a time ...
  In a land far away ...

- Now take it in turns to make up a story, adding to each other's ideas as you go along. When you reach the end, remind the children of familiar endings, e.g.

  And they all lived happily ever after.
  And that was the end of their exciting day.

Tip Try sitting in your role-play area, and using that as the setting for the story.

Cross-curricular link

CD: Developing Imagination and Imaginative Play.

A Bigger Splash by David Hockney

Who jumped in? Children look carefully at a painting, describing what they see and think about it.

Aim

- To give children an opportunity to speak clearly, showing awareness of the listener.

Resources

- A copy of *A Bigger Splash* by David Hockney.

Preparation

- Tell the children they are going to take turns talking about a picture.
- Explain that there are no right or wrong answers.
- Remind them to listen carefully to what others say.

What to do

- Show a group of children the picture, and ask everyone to tell you something they can see in the picture. The children might mention:
  - swimming pool
  - blue sky
  - seats round the pool
  - modern house
  - diving board
  - And the splash!
- Now ask the children to think about the picture. Prompt them with questions such as:

  'How would it feel to be there?'
  'What's the weather like?'
  'What would the water feel like?'

'How was the splash made?'
'Who made the splash?'
'Where are the people?'
'Who lives there?'
'Where do they think this place is?'

- Encourage the children to develop their ideas by asking:

'Why?'
'What makes you think that?'

Vocabulary

splash, spray, dive, diving board, swimming, water, deep, pool, blue, hot, sun, holiday

Tip The children can go on to share their experiences about holidays or swimming.

Cross-curricular link

KUW: Place.

All Aboard by Zoe **Kakolyris**

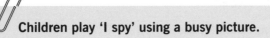

Children play 'I spy' using a busy picture.

Aim

• To provide a stimulating focus for children's discussion.

Resources

• A copy of *All Aboard* by Zoe Kakolyris. See **www.zoes-world.co.uk** for details.

What to do

• Ask the children to look carefully at the picture, choose someone special and work out what they are doing. Start the game by saying, 'I spy a girl doing a handstand, can you see her too?'
• Everyone takes a turn to describe what the person they've chosen is doing.
  The rest of the group should look carefully and try to find the person.
• Now encourage them to speculate:
  – Where is the train going?
  – Where have all the children come from?
  – Can you see any adults? Why not?
  – Can you see any animals?
  – Where is the train driver?
• It may be appropriate to extend the game further:
  Describe your favourite person in the painting by their appearance, e.g.
  – boy or girl?
  – hair?
  – what are they wearing?
  – how old are they?
• Can you think of a name for them?

Vocabulary

jumping, eating, dancing, singing, sitting, walking, talking, laughing, climbing, lying

> **Tip** The children can go on to make a shared picture. Everyone draws a person on a large sheet of paper. *What will your person be doing?*

Cross-curricular link

CD: Being Creative.

Create a character

> The children have fun dressing up in a uniform as you photograph them behind a picture frame.

Aim

- To encourage children to use their own experience of the world.

Resources

- Dressing-up clothes
- An old picture frame
- Camera
- A selection of non-fiction books about people and their jobs
- Access to an Internet provider suitable for Early Years children, e.g. www.espresso.co.uk
- Writing program on a computer, or paper and pens

Preparation

- Read non-fiction books about real people.

What to do

- Working with a small group of children, look together at some of the non-fiction books about people. Use the Internet to find out more about people's work. Do the children know any nurses, doctors, police or firefighters? Encourage them to share their experiences.
- Let the children dress up as someone new. Take it in turns to pose behind the old picture frame. Photograph the children as if they were pictures in the frame. Then encourage them to talk about their character.
  - Who are they?
  - What is their job?

- – Where do they live?
- – How old are they?
- Help them write a sentence about their character, e.g.

    My name is Saskia and I am a firefighter.

    You might want them to do this on the computer or you to act as a scribe. Remember to help them re-read their writing afterwards.
- Create a class book by collecting together several photographs and sentences. The children will enjoy reading it again and again.

Vocabulary

job, work, uniform

 Tip Try to challenge stereotypes when selecting books and information about people and the jobs they do.

Cross-curricular link

PSED: Sense of Community.

Traditional tales

Fun in the role-play area starting from a traditional tale.

Aim

- To provide an opportunity for children to enact stories as the basis for further imaginative play.

Resources

- A copy of any of the traditional tales
- Dressing-up clothes
- Role-play items to match your chosen story

Preparation

- Make some simple adaptations to your role-play area, e.g.
  - Put out three bowls and chairs of different sizes
  - Create a bridge across a strip of blue paper

What to do

- Retell a traditional story to the children, encouraging them to join in with repeated phrases, e.g.

  'I'll huff and I'll puff and I'll blow your house down.'

- Take a small group of children into the prepared role-play area. Ask them who they think might live here.
- Encourage them to use the events of the story in their play. Try taking on a role yourself, e.g.

  'I'm going to sit by this bridge and see who tries to cross it.'

  Pick up the wolf mask and invite the children to be the three pigs while you try to blow their house down.

- Remember to use stories that are relevant to your children; perhaps you might use a scenario from the story of Rama and Sita at Diwali time.

Vocabulary

Language from the different stories

Tip Include opportunities for reading and writing during these story-based activities, e.g. leave a note on the table from Mummy asking Red Riding Hood to take the basket of fruit to Grandma.

Cross-curricular link

CLL: Story events.

The Surprise Party by Pat Hutchins

Play Chinese Whispers with literary phrases from a well-known story.

Aim

- To encourage children to play with language.

Resources

- Hutchins, P. (1993) *The Surprise Party,* London: Red Fox Books.

Preparation

- Read the story to the children to help them appreciate how the message changes.
- Discuss the meaning of some unfamiliar vocabulary, e.g. hoeing the parsley or raiding the poultry.
- Look at how the words I'M HAVING A PARTY are written.

    Is Rabbit still whispering his message?

What to do

- Explain to the children that when you whisper it is not always easy to hear clearly.
  Tell them you're going to play a whispering game where messages are often mixed up and that's part of the fun!
- When everyone is sitting in a circle, the adult whispers one of the phrases from the book to the child on their left, e.g.

    'Rabbit is hoeing the parsley tomorrow'

- That child then whispers the message to the next child, and so on round the circle.

- When the message gets back to the adult she repeats it aloud for everyone to hear.
- Now tell the children what the original message was.
  - Has it changed?

Vocabulary

Phrases from the book

Tip You'll have more fun if you use a complicated phrase which is more likely to be changed than an easily recognisable message like 'I'm having a party tomorrow'.

Cross-curricular link

PSED: Making Relationships.

What's going to happen?

To provide an opportunity for the children to think about stories and speculate about what happens next.

Aim

- To help children to draw conclusions and speculate about the plot of a story.

Resources

- Burningham, J. (1979) *Mr Gumpy's Motorcar*, London: Picture Puffins.
- Burningham, J. (1979) *Mr Gumpy's Outing*, London: Picture Puffins.

Preparation

- Read the stories yourself before discussing them with the children.

What to do

- Read the story of Mr Gumpy's outing in the boat.
  Show the children the picture of everyone in the boat when they were going along happily.
  Ask children to guess what they think will happen next.
- If they suggest the boat will sink, ask them why that might happen, then continue to the end of the story.
- Count up how many people and animals were in the boat before it tipped.
- Look at each picture in turn.
  - Can they remember what Mr Gumpy said to the children and each animal?
  - Why do they think everyone wanted to go in the boat?
  - Would they like to have been there?

- Now show the children the second book about Mr Gumpy. Read the first two pages then ask the children what they think might happen next.
  When they guess that the children and animals will want to join him, carry on with the story.
- Stop reading when they are driving along happily.
  Ask the children what they think might happen.
  They may use ideas from the previous book or they may make other suggestions.
- Read on to the next pages until the rain starts, then ask for the children's ideas:
  - Do they notice that the car has no roof?
  - Does anyone think about what will happen to the track across the field in the rain?
- When the wheels began to spin and Mr Gumpy needs someone to push:
  - Who do the children think will help and why?
- Read on until they get the car going and the sun comes out.
- Tell the children that the ending is not going to be exactly the same as the first story.
  - How do they think the story will end?
- Read to the end.
  - Were you right? Did it end as you thought it would?

Tip This activity can easily be adapted to other books that have one character appearing in both stories.

Cross-curricular link

CCL: Story events.

Nursery rhyme competition

A team game to show how many nursery rhymes your children know.

Aim

- To encourage children to recall and enjoy familiar nursery rhymes.

What to do

- Divide the children into three groups, each with an adult.
  Explain that you are going to have a competition to find out who knows the most nursery rhymes.
  Give each group a number. Group One has to be ready with a nursery rhyme.
- Start by encouraging everyone to count to 10 keeping a steady beat.
  As soon as '10' has been said Group One has to say their nursery rhyme together.
- As soon as they stop they start the count, 1, 2, 3 .....
  When they reach '10', Group Two should immediately say their chosen rhyme.
- Children then start the count to 10 again, which is the signal for Group Three to say their first rhyme.
- Continue in this way, round and round the groups until:
  - One group repeats a rhyme that has already been said, or
  - One group can't think of another rhyme
  That group is now 'out'.
- The competition continues between the other two groups until a winner is declared.
  Everyone can still join in with the counting and the arbitration!

Tip Encourage the children to use any number rhymes and other favourite rhymes that they know.

Cross-curricular link

PSED: Dispositions and Attitudes.

Part 2
Reading

Plan an environment that is rich in signs, symbols, notices, numbers, words, rhymes, books . . . allow plenty of time for children to browse and share these resources with adults and other children.

Practice Guidance for the Early Years Foundation Stage, May 2008, p. 42

Chapter 4
World of books

Candles (1)

> Explore the magic of candlelight as you read books about festivals of light.

Aim

- To encourage children to add to their first-hand experience of the world through books.

Resources

- Books about festivals with a focus on light, e.g.

    Zucker, J. (2002), *Eight Candles to Light: A Chanukah Story*, London: Frances Lincoln
    Zucker, J. (2005), *Lighting a Lamp: A Divali Story*, London: Frances Lincoln
    Zucker, J. (2005), *Lanterns and Firecrackers: A Chinese New Year Story*, London: Frances Lincoln
    Holub, J. (2000) *Light the Candles: A Hannukah Lift-the-flap Book*, London: Picture Puffins

Preparation

- Set up a display within your book area.
- Use a dark fabric to cover a table or drape from a noticeboard.
- Against this, display some candles, candlesticks, lanterns and lamps that represent those used in the different festivals.

What to do

- Plan your reading session for when it is getting dark.
  Switch off the main lights and light a lamp or a candle in your reading area.
  Read one of the books each day.
- Ask the children what they remember about the previous day's story. Encourage the children to compare the different ways that lights are used in these festivals.
  - What do they notice that is the same?
  - When do they light candles at home?
- There are many festivals that feature candles and light when you could introduce this activity – Divali, Hannukah, Christmas, birthdays.

Vocabulary

light, lamp, lantern, candle

Tip If you want to light a candle, only do so when the children are all seated quietly with you. Stand your candle in a metal biscuit tin that has been filled with sand, and place it on a firm surface out of the children's reach. Have your fire blanket close by you. Pass the matches to another adult to put away as soon as you have used them.

Cross-curricular link

KUW: Communities.

Candles (2)

> The children read a rhyme together then adapt it to their own names.

Aim

- To encourage children to begin to 'read' by themselves.

Resources

- Book containing the nursery rhyme *Jack Be Nimble*
- A large version of the rhyme

Preparation

- Say the rhyme together so that the children become familiar with it, and maybe learn to say it themselves.

What to do

- Say the rhyme together and add some actions.

    Jack be nimble – dance around on tiptoes
    Jack be quick – stand on the spot and jog as fast as you can
    Jack jump over the candlestick – jump up high

- Sit together and look at your large version of the rhyme.
  Draw the children's attention to the layout of a poem on the page.
  Did they notice that each line is short?
- Say the rhyme together, with you pointing to the words.
  Sometimes, you keep quiet and let the children supply the next word.
  Individual children might like to come out and read it out loud to the group.
- Now form a circle.

Hold hands and sing and act it again, but with a different name each time, e.g.

All be nimble
All be quick
'Freddie' jump over the candlestick

Listen for your name. Only that child jumps into the centre of the circle of children.

Vocabulary

nimble, quick

Tip Make an old-fashioned candlestick from cardboard tubes and a paper plate and use this in the centre of the circle for children to jump over.

Cross-curricular link

PD: Movement and Space.

Candles (3)

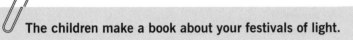

The children make a book about your festivals of light.

Aim

- To create a class book that the children can read.

Resources

- Camera
- Printer
- Photograph album

Preparation

- Take photographs of the children with any candles, lamps, lanterns, etc. that they have used during a festival shared in their home.
  - You could borrow the light from the family and take the photograph in your setting.
  - You could borrow a photograph from home.

What to do

- Help the children to place one photograph on each page of the album.
- Encourage the children to create a short sentence about their own picture and help them to write it, or write it for them.
  Cut out the sentence and fix it in the album next to the photograph.
- Decide together on a suitable title and make a front cover and add the book to your candle display.
  Read the book together.
  Individual children could read their own page to the group.
- When you have changed your display, keep it in your book-box so that the children have access to it, and can read it whenever they choose.

Vocabulary

children's names, festival names

 Tip If you use an album with a sticky plastic sheet over each page, it makes it easy for the children to mount their own work.

Cross-curricular link

PSED: Sense of Community.

All the little ducks

Work with the children to set up a springtime display featuring ducks.

Aim

- To enable the children to experience a range of books on one topic.

Resources

- Books about ducks
- Display board and surface area
- Yellow fabric or paper
- Pictures and models of ducks

Preparation

- Cover the display board with appropriate paper. Yellow is an obvious choice. Display some pictures of ducks and the words of 'Five Little Ducks' (See 'Five Little Ducks' activity on page 314 in Chapter 9: Making a Book)
- Find four or five books about ducks. You could even put some yellow cushions in your book area to continue the yellow theme.

What to do

- Show the children your chosen books about ducks. Stand them on the shelf, or on a table in your book area. Make sure that the children can reach them.
- Over the week, read all of these books to the children. Encourage the children to read/look at the books themselves.
- Children can add other duck books to the collection – ones from your book area or ones from home.
- Children can add their own drawings and paintings of ducks to the wall display, bring in toy ducks or make models of ducks to stand on the shelf with the books.

Tip Include some non-fiction books as well as stories and rhymes.

Cross-curricular link

KUW: Exploration and Investigation.

How to . . .

Help the children to create some recipe books by taking photographs as you cook.

Aim

- To help children learn that information can be retrieved from books.

Resources

- Digital camera
- Sticky labels

Preparation

- Decide what you are going to cook, and collect ingredients and utensils.
- Share some recipe books with the children so that they start to recognise their use.

What to do

- At each stage of your cooking process choose one child to take a photograph.
  Aim to have:
  - The ingredients
  - Children putting aprons on
  - Each stage of cooking
  - Washing up/tidying away
  - The finished food
- Help the children to print out the photos.
  Lay them out so that everyone can see them.
  Are they in the right order?

- Ask the children to sort the photographs into the correct sequence. Explain why this is important.

  'What would happen if you cooked this in the wrong order?'

- Now, punch holes in them and tie them together.

  Help the children to form a simple sentence for each picture. Scribe it onto a sticky label, then each child can stick one onto the relevant photograph.

  What's missing? A title, or cover.

  Children can make this and add it to their book of instructions.

 Tip Do this each time you cook to build up a recipe section in your children's book corners. Perhaps they could borrow a recipe and take it home to try making it again..

Cross-curricular link

KUW: ICT.

Holidays (1)

Make a collection of postcards from holiday destinations, sort these into sets with the children and create a display.

Aim

- To create an environment for your children that is rich in print using labels and books.

Resources

- A collection of postcards

Preparation

- Talk to the children about holidays and day trips out.
  Ask where they have been.
- Encourage them to bring in postcards of places they have visited.
  Put up a notice for the parents and allow a few days to collect all contributions.

What to do

- When you have a good collection of postcards spread them out on the floor.
  Let a small group of children explore the images on the cards.
  Use this as another opportunity for talking and sharing experiences.
- Then using sorting rings or large sheets of paper sort the postcards into three or four sets. Ideas could include: seaside, hotel, theme park or village.
  Encourage the children to make decisions about sorting, and be accepting of their ideas.
- Ask the children for suggestions for a label for each set. What should it be?
  Let the children watch as you write out some appropriate labels for their sets.

- Display the postcards in their sets.
  Now get the children to find books that link to their sets and add these to your display. Try to include both fiction and non-fiction books.
- Encourage other children to come and look at the display.
  Explain that the postcards have been sorted into sets.
  - Can they read the labels or work out what they might say?

Vocabulary

seaside, mountain, lake, town, village, hotel, pool, theme park

Tip   Read some of these books during story time.

Cross-curricular links

PSRN: Calculating.

My tune

Children compose and read their own music.

Aim

- To provide an opportunity for children to practise tracking symbols from left to right.

Resources

- Strips of paper
- Sticky circles
- Instruments

Preparation

- Fold each strip of paper into four sections to make a line.

What to do

- Give each child a strip of paper and three sticky circles. Explain to the children:

  'You can stick one of your circles into one of the sections of your paper. Choose any section you like.'

  'Now stick another circle in another section, and the third circle in a different section.'

  'You should have three sections with circles, and one empty section.'

| | | • | • | | • | • | • |

- Explain to the children:

  'When you see a circle you will play your instrument.'
  'When the section is empty you will rest.'

  Demonstrate with an instrument so everyone understands.
- Using a percussion instrument the children will now play their own piece of music.
  Starting at the left and moving along to the right of the strip of paper, the child will play one beat for each circle, and rest for the space.
- You count a strong, 1-2-3-4 rhythm to help them keep time.
  Several children can all play their own tunes at the same time, as you count.
- Once they are familiar with this process let the children:
  - swap strips with a friend, or
  - turn their strip round and play the new tune.

Variations for more able children

- Place the strips one under the other and play a longer tune. An adult can point to each strip in turn to keep children together.
- Make some strips that have eight sections and six circles.

Tip If you want to use chime bars, let the children choose from C, G, D, A, E. These form the pentatonic scale and will always harmonise.

Cross-curricular link

CD: Creating Music and Dance.

Story places

Using picture books that fit in with your theme to help your children think about settings for stories.

Aim

- To help children begin to be aware that stories have settings.

Resources

- Several story books on your chosen theme, e.g. setting: in the garden.
  Use, e.g. Butterworth, N. and Inkpen, M. (2006) *Jasper's Beanstalk*, London: Hodder Children's Books;
  Carle, E. (2002) *The Very Hungry Caterpillar*, London: Puffin Books;
  Carle, E. (2009) *The Tiny Seed*, London: Simon & Schuster Children's;
  French, V. and Bartlett, A. (1995) *Oliver's Vegetables*, London: Hodder Children's Books.

What to do

- Show the children the chosen story books and remind the children of the stories.
- Take one of the books and ask the children where the story happens. Repeat this for the other books.

    'Who notices anything?'
    'All of these books take place in . . .'

- Explain that this is called the 'setting'. It is where the story happens. Think about what you might find in this setting, e.g. in the garden you may find flowers, beetles, swings or a sandpit.
- What about other settings? What do you think you might find if the story was set in . . .

    . . . the forest: wolf, trees, birds
    . . . the sea: mermaids, shells, fish
    . . . a house: mummy, bed, television

- Can the children think of any books with these settings?

  Children may be able to look through your book box to find
  something they remember that has one of these settings.
  Read some of these books each day.
  Leave them out together so that children can look at them
  whenever they want to.

Vocabulary

setting

Tip Your starting point could be any theme/setting which fits with your
current work.

Cross-curricular link

CLL: Story setting.

My grandma

Make a collection of books for the children to think about their own grandma.

Aim

- To encourage children to add their own experience of the world.

Resources

- A copy of *Little Red Riding Hood*.
- Other stories that feature grandmas, e.g.
  Hedderwick, M. (2010) *Katie Morag and the Two Grandmothers*, London: Red Fox Books;
  Butterwick, N. (2008) *My Grandma is Wonderful*, London: Walker Books;
  Exley, H. (2006) *Me and My Grandma*, Watford: Exley Publications.

Preparation

- Ask the children to collect books that have a grandma in them.

What to do

- Ask the children to retell the story of Little Red Riding Hood.
  Show them a picture of the grandma in your copy of the story.
- Let the children look at the pictures in other books and find pictures of grandmas.
  Ask the children if they've got a grandma (be sensitive to alternative names).
  Collect names they call their grandma, e.g. Nana, Granny . . .
- What's special about their grandma?
  - What is she like?
  - What does she do for them?
  - Does she come to visit them?
  - Does she look like a grandma in the story books?

What do they like doing with their grandma?
Can they walk from their house to grandma's house like Red Riding Hood does?

- Do the children understand the relationship between them and their grandma, e.g.
  - Is she Daddy's mum or Mummy's mum?
  - Can they tell you if they are a granddaughter or a grandson?
  Perhaps you could show photographs of you as a child with your grandma.
- Type out and display all the alternative names for 'Grandma' (see Tip).
  Display them with the story books you have collected.
- If the children are keen to explore this further, maybe you could make a book collection about grandads too.

Vocabulary

Grandma, Granny, Nana, Nannie

Tip

Display the names used for 'Grandma' in the languages spoken by families in your setting to raise awareness of different languages and scripts, e.g.

Mamie (French), Abuela (Spanish), Oma (German), Babcia (Polish)

Cross-curricular link

KUW: Time.

Books at home

Everyone reads the books they have taken home and votes for their favourite.

Aim

- To emphasise the importance of parents reading with children.

Resources

- A collection of books, e.g. books about bears.
- A3 sheets of paper showing the title of each book, one book per sheet.
- Stickers in three colours.

Preparation

- Select a set of seven or eight books linked by a theme.
- Display a notice informing parents about the special books on loan this week.
- Make an attractive display with the books for children to choose from.
- Put the A3 sheets in an accessible position for children to record which book they have borrowed.

What to do

- Collect a group of children together to look at the books. Let them handle the books and talk about those they know and those they'd like to read.
- Tell them they can take one of these books home for their parent to read with them. Explain that you are going to find out which books most people enjoy best.
- Help the children choose a book each for taking home and write their name under the book's title on the A3 sheet.

- Next day, encourage parents and children to select a sticker to indicate their opinion of the book they have read, e.g.

   green: excellent – really enjoyed
   yellow: good – worth reading
   red: OK – not my favourite

- Then introduce the books to another group of children. Repeat the activity until everyone has taken at least one book home.
- Encourage the children to count up the coloured stickers collected for each book. Which one is the class favourite?

Vocabulary

excellent, really enjoyed, worth reading, recommend, favourite, interesting

Tip

Try to provide dual-language books to match the language spoken in the home, and be sensitive to the fact that not all families are literate – you can always do this activity with helpers in the setting if that is more appropriate.

Cross-curricular link

PSED: Self-confidence and Self-esteem.

Who said that?

Using traditional stories to introduce your children to speech bubbles.

Aim

- To create a display that encourages children to learn about print and talk about stories.

Resources

- A selection of familiar story books, e.g. traditional tales.
- Large speech bubbles cut from A3 pieces of paper.

Preparation

- Write in the speech bubbles some repeated phrases used by characters, e.g.

    What big eyes you've got, Grandma
    Who's been eating my porridge?
    Little pig, little pig, let me come in
    Someone's been eating my porridge and it's all gone!

- Display these in your book area with the selection of books close by. Use the words 'Who said that?' as a title for your display.

What to do

- Collect together a small group of children. Ask them if they know what speech bubbles are. Some children may recognise them from cartoon stories or comics.
- Explain that speech bubbles show you the words people say. Tell them that these speech bubbles are from stories they know. Point to the title words as you ask – 'I wonder if anyone will know who said that?'

- Now read one of the speech bubbles together.

  'Can anyone think who said that?'

  Read the other speech bubbles together and establish the character and story.
- Encourage the children to find the characters in the story books provided. Help them display these with the speech bubbles.
- Can anyone think of a different example of speech from one of the stories? If possible, extend your display with your children's suggestions.

Vocabulary

speech bubble, talk, words, say, said, character

Tip Pointing at the words as you read the displayed words will help the children recall the words and encourage them to join in.

Cross-curricular link

CLL: Story characters.

We're going to the zoo

Help the children to choose and photocopy their own version of a story.

Aim

- To help the children develop an understanding of the structure of stories.

Resources

- Prepared pages of a story (see Preparation).
- Access to a photocopier.

Preparation

- On individual sheets of A4 paper write:

  an opening sentence, e.g. *One fine day we all went to the zoo.*
  a closing sentence, e.g. *And we all went home for tea.*
  and several pages with the name of an animal, possibly a picture and a number, e.g. *two elephants*

  For older children, have a choice of opening and closing sentences.
- Put each sheet into a plastic wallet and store in a ringbinder.

What to do

- Explain to the children that they are going to make their own story.

  'What's a good way to start a story?'
  Listen to their suggestions.

- With the children, photocopy today's beginning and give them each their own copy. Help the children to read it.
- Now look at the collection of animal pages.

  'Who can read what they say?'
  Encourage all of the children to have a go.

- They need to choose three of the animal pages and photocopy them.
  Add these to their opening sentence to begin to make a book.
- Now talk about the fact that stories have to end.

  'Who can think of some endings?'
  Photocopy and hand out today's ending. Read it together.

- Fix all your pages together to make your own book.
- On another day, repeat this process to make a different story, e.g.
  We're going on a picnic and we'll take . . . and gradually build up your
  resource file of story ideas.

Tip   Keep the pages in the plastic covering when the children are
photocopying to protect the master copies.

Cross-curricular link

KUW: ICT.

Who am I?

Photograph the children dressed up as story-book characters and make an appropriate speech bubble to display alongside.

Aim

- To encourage children to retell narratives and discuss characters.

Resources

- A selection of familiar stories e.g. traditional tales.
- Dressing-up clothes.
- Camera.
- Paper for speech bubbles or writing program on a computer.

Preparation

- Introduce the children to speech bubbles using the activity 'Who said that?', p. 132
- Make sure the children are familiar with the stories in your selection.

What to do

- Work with a small group of children.
  Ask them to choose a favourite story from the selection.
  Encourage the children to retell one of their favourite stories.
  Can they tell you the main events of the story in sequence?
- Let them dress up as one of the characters and talk about their chosen character.
  Take a photograph of the child dressed up.
- Now tell each child they must think of something that their character says in the story.

Help them choose a well-known or repeated phrase.

> **Either** let the children help you type the words onto the computer, then print the character's words and cut them into a speech bubble.
> **Or** let the children watch you write their words onto a paper speech bubble.

- Display the speech bubble next to the child's photograph.
  Can the other children guess which story-book character they are?

- Use the words 'Who am I?' as a title for your display.

Vocabulary

dialogue from your chosen stories

Tip Choose stories that are suitable for your class and reflect their cultural diversity.

Cross-curricular link

CLL: Story characters.

Outdoor reading

Take your book corner outside on a fine day.

Aim

- To create an attractive book area where children and adults can enjoy books together.

Resources

- Cushions
- Blankets
- Books
- Movable book trolley, unit, shelf or boxes

What to do

- Tell the children that it's such a fine day that you think it would be fun to make a book corner outside.
- Take a small group of children outside to talk about the best area to use. Encourage the children to justify their ideas and listen to each other's suggestions.

    'Do we want it to in the sun? Why not?'
    'What about sitting on the path? Would it be comfortable?'
    'Do we want to be near the bikes or the doorway? Would it be safe?'
    'What about under the tree or canopy? Is it a quiet place?'

- When you have chosen the best place, help the children plan what they need and, if possible, involve the children in moving things outside. Let the children put the items in place to make it a comfortable, safe place to read. Do they want any special rules about how to use the books outside?
- Then let them sit down and enjoy the books.

Vocabulary

cushion, blanket, trolley, box, unit, shelf, book

 Tip Make time for the group who have set up the book area to tell the other children about it.

Cross-curricular link:

PSED: Behaviour and Self-control.

Bookmarks (1)

Make a bookmark to help your children keep their place as they read.

Aim

- To create a resource to help children with their reading.

Resources

- Glitter
- Laminating sheets and laminator

What to do

- Help the children to sprinkle glitter onto a sheet of laminating film. Fold over the top sheet and laminate according to your own equipment.
- Cut this into strips which can be used as bookmarks. Keep them in an attractive pot near your books for anyone to use.
- Sit with a group of children. Make sure that each child has a book and a bookmark.
- Practise using the bookmark to point to the words you are reading. Use this time to reinforce reading from left to right, and moving from the top to the bottom of the page.

Tip Because these bookmarks are almost transparent they don't hinder the children who are able to 'read ahead'. They can still see the next word or spot that the sentence continues onto the next line.

Cross-curricular link

KUW: Designing and Making.

Bookmarks (2)

 Children make their own special lolly stick bookmark.

Aim

- To create a personal marker and encourage children to read.

Resources

- Lolly sticks
- Variation 1: Felt-tip pens; Variation 2: Scraps of felt and wool, and old gloves

What to do

- Choose which idea to use with your children today.

Variation 1 – for children who can write their own names:

- Help the children to write their name along the length of the lolly stick using the felt-tip pens. Practise on a piece of scrap paper, if necessary.
- Leave a little space at the end of their name, where they can add a small drawing, e.g. a flower, flag or car.

Variation 2 – involves making a finger puppet:

- Cut the fingers from the gloves and give one to each child. These should be 2–3 cm long.
- Help the children to stick features onto their finger puppet, e.g.
  - black spots onto a red finger to make a ladybird
  - two large eyes on a green finger to make a frog
  - nose, eyes and mouth with some wool hair, to make a face.
- Push the lolly stick inside the finger puppet and glue in place.

 Tip Children can use their lolly stick bookmarks to identify the book they have chosen to take home today.

Cross-curricular link

KUW: Designing and Making.

Chapter 5
Finding out

Garden centre (2)

Using labels to identify the parts of a sunflower and help children read.

Aim

- To help children understand the concept of a word.

Resources

- Carle, E. (2009) *The Tiny Seed*, London: Simon & Schuster Children's
- A pot of sunflowers
- Yellow and green tissue paper, PVA glue, edible seeds (e.g. pumpkin seeds)
- Some large, and some small, labels cut from card

Preparation

- Read and enjoy the story of *The Tiny Seed* by Eric Carle. Look carefully and think how Eric Carle might have created the pictures in it.
- Allow time for the children to look carefully at the sunflowers. Can they identify the different parts of the plants?

What to do

- Work as a group to create a huge sunflower collage for your wall. Ask the children to identify each part of the flower in turn. Write the word clearly on a label and stick it next to the flower part with removable adhesive.
- Read the labels together. Look at the initial letter for each one as you do so.
- Remove the labels, mix them up and hand them out to the children. Ask each one in turn to read their label and tell you where it goes. Stick them back up. Repeat until everyone has had a turn. Start with your more able children to give the others a chance to learn or remember what the labels say.

- Leave out some sets of small labels using the same words so that children can choose to make small collage flowers and stick on labels. These could be used in your Garden Centre role play or as a 'catalogue' of different flowers that the customers could buy.

Vocabulary

stem, leaf, bud, flower, seeds

Tip The arrangement of seeds in a sunflower is quite complicated. Point it out to the children but don't expect them to be able to repeat it in their own work.

Cross-curricular link

KUW: Exploration and Investigation.

What's in your name?

Have fun with this letter recognition game as the children respond to the letters in their names by stepping towards the leader.

Aim

- To help the children remember the letters in their name.

Resources

- A set of plastic letters in a bag – as long as you have all the ones in this group of children's names you may not want to use all 26 letters of the alphabet.
- Scrap paper for writing their names.

Preparation

- Check that everyone knows the letters in their own name.
- The children can write them out to take with them when they play the game in case they need to check.

What to do

- Choose someone to be the leader. This adult or child stands at the front with the bag of letters. The other children line up facing the leader, about six or seven strides away.
- The leader reaches into a bag and picks out a letter at random. Do they know the letter's name? If not, be ready to help.
- The leader then calls out the letter's name and holds it up for everyone to see. If any child has that letter in their name they take one stride forward towards the leader.

'If you have two of this letter, you take two strides.'

- The leader continues picking and calling out letter names. The first child to reach the leader takes over as leader. Everyone else returns to the base line.

 Tip An adult needs to monitor the game for accuracy and to help those who are still learning how to spell their own name.

Cross-curricular link

PSED: Making Relationships.

Breakfast time

Using cereal boxes to help children recognise words and symbols.

Aim

- To encourage the children to recall words or symbols that they see frequently.

Resources

- Cereal packets
- Pictures of cereal plants or containers of seeds: use oats, rice, wheat and corn
- Hoops and labels

Preparation

- Set out hoops with one picture or container of grain and the appropriate label in each.

What to do

- Spend some time looking at the cereal packets. Can the children identify the different cereals by their packaging and labelling? Talk about, e.g.
  - which one you like best
  - which one you had today
  - which one you've never tasted
- Show the children the pictures of cereal plants or the containers of seeds from the plants. Explain to them that the cereals in the packets are made from the seeds/grains of these plants.

- Look at and identify one of the plants, e.g. rice.
  Can the children suggest which cereals might be made from rice? The clue is usually in the name. Help the children to spot this. Find the boxes that are made from rice and place them in the 'rice' hoop.
- Repeat for the other cereals.

Vocabulary

oats, wheat, rice, corn

Tip You could make a display with your boxes, or use them in your shop.

Cross-curricular link

PSRN: Calculating.

Carnival head-dresses

Children make their own hat to wear during a carnival parade.

Aim

- To help children carry out an activity by reading the instructions.

Resources

- Card or strong paper long enough to fit a child's head
- Collage material, including long lengths of ribbon, flowers, sequins and glitter
- Sticky tape and glue

Preparation

- Write out three instructions at a level to match the children's abilities.
- Use a diagram, or a diagram with labels, or short, clear, simple sentences.

  1. Choose a band.
  2. Decorate the band.
  3. Fix the ends together.

What to do

- Read the instructions to the children or ask them to tell you what they say.
  Can they work out the correct order for the instructions?
  Fix the instruction sheets in order, where the children can see them as they work.
- Check that the children understand the instructions.
  They can now make their own hat using these simple instructions.
  Keep asking the children which instruction they are working on.
- When they are finished ask the children to check that they have completed all of the instructions.

Vocabulary

instruction

 Tip Make sure that the children decorate their bands with items that will flow and float in the air as they dance in the parade.

Cross-curricular link

KUW: Designing and Making.

Where are we?

> Go for a walk with the children and photograph all the familiar signs you see in the street.

Aim

- To provide an opportunity for children to recognise words on signs and symbols.

Resources

- Digital camera and printer

Preparation

- You are going to be taking the children out of the setting, so prepare well in advance, keeping to the rules of your setting for doing this.
- Look around the local area so that you can plan the best route for spotting signs and symbols.

What to do

- Go for a walk with the children in the streets around your setting.
- Take photographs of any signs that let you know where you are. Try:
  - Street names
  - Directions to town, the theatre, etc.
  - The board with your own setting's name on it
  - Similar boards for schools or churches
  - Names of shops, factories, garages, businesses
- Look out for familiar logos, e.g.
  - Bus stop
  - Road signs showing children crossing
  - Takeaway restaurants

- On returning, the children can work with an adult to print out their photographs.
- Can the children read or recognise any of the signs? Provide clues – the first letter if that is helpful. (It is helpful for '**M**ain Street'. It isn't helpful for '**Sh**oreditch'.)
  The children may recognise logos for fast food outlets, car dealerships and petrol stations etc.

Vocabulary

direction, sign, logo

Tip You could create a display by cutting up an old street map to make mounts for your photographs or as a trim to go round the edge of your display board.

Cross-curricular link

KUW: Place.

Birthday (3)

Teddy's having a birthday party and he sends invitations to everyone. Help the children to read their invitation from Teddy.

Aim

- To provide some simple texts which children can decode.

Resources

- Party invitations and envelopes

Preparation

- Select a party invitation either printed from a computer program or some simple, bought paper invitations.
- Fill out an invitation for every child from Teddy.
- Put the invitations in a named envelope for each child.

What to do

- Show the children the envelopes that have been left in the classroom. Let them collect the envelope addressed to them if they recognise their name. Less able children might be able to select their name from a group of three or four.
- Working in small groups, encourage the children to open their envelopes and find out what's inside. Who can recognise that it's an invitation to a birthday party?
- Encourage the children to try to read who it is from.

    'It's Teddy's birthday and he's having a party.'

- Then try to work out the day and the time of the party.

  'How old will Teddy be?'

- Make the party for the following day so the children can read their invitations with their parents at home too.

Vocabulary

envelope, name, party, Teddy, Monday/Tuesday/Wednesday/Thursday/Friday, one/two/three o'clock

 Tip For older children you could help them to find Teddy's birthday on a calendar. Do they know when their birthday is?

Cross-curricular link

PSRN: Numbers as Labels and for Counting.

Catch That Goat! by Polly Alakija (1)

> Look at the illustrations in this super book. Then help the children to create their own market stall.

Aim

- To encourage children to use illustrations to find out information from a book.

Resources

- Alakija, P. (2007) *Catch That Goat!: A Market Day in Nigeria*, Bath: Barefoot Books
- Paper and paint
- Tables and role-play resources

Preparation

- Read and enjoy the story.

What to do

- Spend time looking at the illustrations to work out what the different market traders are selling. Use the shop signs, noting both the words and the images. Look at the goods on display for additional clues.
- Now make your own market.
  - Arrange the tables in a line.
  - Use class or nursery resources such as model fruit and vegetables, packets from the shop, plates, etc. from the house, dressing-up clothes and musical instruments to fill your market stalls.
- Children can work in pairs to paint a sign for their stall. They could try forming the word or use a symbol. Help the children to tape their sign across the front of their table/stall.
- Your market is now ready for role-play use.

Vocabulary

market, stall, market trader

Tip If you have a street market nearby, visit it before you start this activity.

Cross-curricular link

KUW: Communities.

New for old

Replace the old labels in your room and remind the children of the routines involved as they make new ones.

Aim

- To create an environment for the children that is rich in print.

Resources

- Digital camera
- Printer
- Laminator

What to do

- Ask the children to have a look at the different labels that are up in the room. Do they notice that they are torn, damaged, grubby, etc.? Explain to them that it is time to change these labels for some new ones.
- Tell the children that you are going to use photographs and words to give information, or to act as reminders about how to behave or use the resources. Discuss the possibilities.
  Be ready with some ideas to help the children, e.g.

  Photograph: someone's hands in a basin with the tap running and soap all over their hands
  Words: 'Wash your hands'
  Where will it go?

  Photograph: someone sweeping the floor near the sand tray
  Words: 'Clear away when you have finished'
  Where will it go?

  Photograph: child wearing an apron
  Words: 'You need to wear an apron'
  Where will it go?

- Now, take the photographs with the children. Let them do as much as possible of this.
- Write out the words and let the children copy them on the computer. Laminate and then put up your new labels.

Vocabulary

label, information

Tip This is a good activity for the beginning of any term as it is a chance to reinforce your setting's routines.

Cross-curricular link

PSED: Behaviour and Self-control.

Bags of words

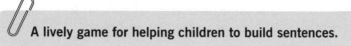

A lively game for helping children to build sentences.

Aim

- To provide an opportunity for children to read a range of words and simple sentences.

Resources

- Six carrier bags in different colours, labelled 1–6
- A large die
- Strips of card numbered 1–6
- A selection of simple sentences linked to your theme, using five words each, e.g.
  - I can play the drum/triangle/guitar
  - I like to eat pizza/chips/cakes
  - I can see the bat/ball/cat/house
  - I am in the car/house/room/bed

Note that the final word in each sentence should be different each time.

Preparation

- Cut each sentence into five separate words and a full stop. Put the first word of each sentence into the bag numbered 1, the second words into the bag numbered 2 and so on. Put all the full stops in bag 6.
- Hook the bags up all around the grounds of your setting.

What to do

- Everyone sits in a circle outside. Give each child a strip of paper numbered 1–6 on which to place their sentence pieces as they collect them.

1	2	3	4	5	6

- The first child rolls the large die in the centre of the circle and reads the number.
  They have to run to find the bag that has that number on it and collect a word – or a full stop.
- If a child already has that number they pass.
  Make this fun, e.g.

    The child has to stand up and stamp that number of times on the floor before handing the die on to their neighbour.

- Continue until everyone has a sentence. Now read them to each other.

Vocabulary

- Any words that you are focusing on in your reading or writing

Tip Use words you want the children to recognise in their reading. Laminate them if you want to reuse the activity.

Cross-curricular link

PSRN: Numbers as Labels and for Counting.

Mini-beasts (3)

Write out the children's questions on bookmarks to encourage them to hunt for information in simple non-fiction books.

Aim

- To reinforce and apply children's reading ability whilst retrieving information from non-fiction texts.

Resources

- Non-fiction books about mini-beasts
- Strips of card

Preparation

- At the start of the new topic ask the children what they would like to find out about mini-beasts. Form their ideas into simple questions.
- Write each question along the length of the strip of card, e.g.
  - Are all ladybirds red and black?
  - How many legs has a spider got?
- Now place one card, like a bookmark, in a non-fiction book at the page that you know contains the answer.

What to do

- Place a crate of non-fiction books, with their bookmark questions, outside.
- Children work in pairs to choose a book. Help them to read the question and then hunt for the answer on the page indicated.
- Encourage children to scan the page for key words, e.g. *spider, legs*.

- Help them to read the relevant sentence, recognising familiar words. Now, talk about the meaning.
- Leave paper and pencils and crayons available so that children can record their information whilst you help another two children with reading their question.

Vocabulary

how? what? where? when? why?

Tip Write the title and page number on the back of the bookmark so that you can replace them quickly when someone has helpfully tidied them all away for you!

Cross-curricular link

KUW: Exploration and Investigation.

Treasure hunt clues

This game makes reading exciting as the children follow the clues to find the treasure.

Aim

- To help children rapidly decode words.

Resources

- Simple clues written on pieces of card using vocabulary that your children are learning to recognise – no more than six clues, e.g.
  - Look behind the door
  - Look under the car mat
  - Look near the sand toys
  - Look in the book box
- Treasure – fruit snack for the day/a lost toy/a new toy/a new book for story time.

Preparation

- Put the cards in place behind the named items and hide the final treasure.
- Remember to keep the first clue to start the game.
- Include outdoor clues if the weather is fine.

What to do

- Working with a group of children, tell the children what treasure they are going to hunt, e.g.

  To find today's snack

- Explain the game so the children understand how to follow the clues. Read the first clue together, e.g.

  Look behind the door

  Let the children start the hunt.
  When they discover the correct door, they will find the second clue card.
- Let the children retrieve the next clue from its hiding place.
  - Who can read the clue?
- This will lead them to the next object hiding a clue card.
- Continue until all the clues have been found and read.
- When the treasure is found, share it with the rest of the class.

Vocabulary

look, behind, on top of, under

Tip

When the children are familiar with the treasure hunt game you can introduce more challenging clues that involve guessing, e.g.

Look behind something tall and red.

Cross-curricular link

PSRN: Shape, Space and Measures.

Key word bingo

Chalk some words in grids on your playground and create a fun way to practise key words outdoors.

Aim

- To develop children's grapheme correspondence so that they can rapidly decode words.

Resources

- Chalk
- Set of key words (see vocabulary list opposite)
- A fine day!

Preparation

- Draw two grids on a hard surface outside – each with six sections.
- Write one of the key words in each section of the two grids.
- Make sure you have these twelve key words in your set of key word cards.

What to do

- Divide the children into two teams of six and let them stand near their grid. Explain the game of bingo to the children if they haven't played it before.
- Show everyone a key word card.
  - Who can read it?
  - Is that word on your grid?
  If it's there, one of the children stands on that word on their grid.
- Then show the next word.
  - Who can read it?
  - Is it on your grid?

- Continue until all of one team are standing on all six words on their grid. They are the winners!
- Swap the teams around and play again with a different grid. Can anyone read all the words on their new grid?

Vocabulary

twelve high-frequency words taken from Letters and Sounds: Appendix 1, e.g. the, and, a, to, said, in, he, I, of, it, was, you

 Tip Have some extra key words in your set that are not on the grids to add further interest.

Cross-curricular link

CLL: Reading a range of simple words.

Guess who! (1)

Children will enjoy reading their names as they play this game.

Aim

- To help children understand what a word is by using names.

Resources

- Name labels

Preparation

- Make sure everyone knows the names of all the children in the class.

What to do

- Sit in a circle with all the name labels in the centre.
- Ask the children what the words are.
  - Do they recognise them as names?
  - Can they spot their own name?
- The children take turns to find their own name and take it back to their place in the circle. When everyone has their name label, hold them up so they can be seen.
- Choose a child to put their name back in the centre. Let that child choose the next one to put their name label back. Continue around the circle until everyone has returned their label.
- Now let the first child pick up someone else's name.
  - Can they read the word?
  - What sound does the word begin with?
  - Does that sound match the first letter written?

- When the child has read the name they can give it to the owner of the name label.
  Now take turns until everyone has retrieved and read someone else's label.
  Save the name labels to play with again another day.

Vocabulary

children's names

Tip Use this activity to apply children's developing phonic knowledge.

Cross-curricular link

PSED: Sense of Community.

Guess who! (2)

Take photographs of pairs of children facing away from the camera. Can the children recognise one another from their back view?

Aim

- To help children understand what a word is by using names.

Resources

- Name labels
- Camera

Preparation

- Make sure everyone knows the names of all the children in the class.

What to do

- Work with a small group for this activity. Have name labels for that group.
- Begin by discussing having your photograph taken.

    What do you usually do?
    Well, today you're NOT going to look at the camera and smile, you're going to turn your back!

- Let two children stand together showing their backs to the rest of the group.

    Do you think you still know who it is?
    How can you tell who is who?

Encourage the children to talk about height and the clothes they are wearing. Consider hair colour and length as well. Find the name labels for these children, and then repeat the activity with different pairs of children.

- Ask the children to choose a partner who looks different from them. Now take photographs of each pair with their backs turned. If possible, let the children watch as the photographs are printed.
- Display the photographs so they are accessible to the children. Put reusable adhesive on the back of the name labels and leave them near by.
- Encourage the children to match the names to the photographs. Let other children in the group try naming the photographs.

Vocabulary

children's names

 Tip **Next day, put the labels next to the wrong photographs and let the children sort them out.**

Cross-curricular link

PSED: Sense of Community.

Key word tunnels

Take a group of children outside for a ball game that includes reading practice.

Aim

- To provide an opportunity for children to read some familiar words.

Resources

- A set of enlarged cards of the key words you are working on
- Container
- Ball

Preparation

- Put the key word cards in the container so that they can't be read.
- Take it outside with you.

What to do

- Choose three children to make the tunnels. They should stand in a line facing the other children with their legs wide apart, but with the sides of their feet touching the feet of the child next to them. They form three 'tunnels' with their open legs.

- Each of these three children picks a card from the container as you hand it to them.
  They should hold their cards so that the other children **can't** read them yet.
- The remaining children form a line. The first child comes forward and rolls a ball through one of the 'tunnels'.
  - Which one will it go through?
- If it goes through a tunnel, that child holds up their key word card.
  - Can the child who rolled the ball read it?
- If they can, they swap places with the child making that tunnel.
- Before getting into place as a 'tunnel', they should pick another key word card from the container.
- A helpful child can retrieve the ball while the original card is replaced in the container, amongst the other cards. The child who made the tunnel goes to the end of the line of those children waiting to roll the ball.

Vocabulary

Any key words such as I, on, the, and, here, is

Tip   Putting the cards back into play means that there is a chance to reinforce learning and support any children who find this task difficult.

Cross-curricular link

PD: Movement and Space.

Key words of the week

The children cut and stick key words from newspaper headlines that you have selected.

Aim

- To help children recognise some key words.

Resources

- A4 paper
- Scissors, glue
- Headlines and titles from newspapers, magazines and leaflets
- Set of key words

Preparation

- Cut out headlines or other bold, clear print from the newspapers etc. Check that they contain the key words you want to practise and that the content is suitable for young children.
- Set out scissors, glue, paper and key words.

What to do

- Show the children one of the key words and read it together.
- Share out some of the magazine cuttings.
- Ask the children if they can find this same key word there.
- The children can now cut out the word and stick it onto one of the sheets of paper. You should end up with a set of papers, each with one key word on it in various fonts, sizes, and colours, arranged all over the paper.
- When everyone has stuck on their word, read the paper together.
- Everyone reads their own word when the adult points to it. Of course, they are all the same!

- Repeat this activity for the other key words.

  You may decide to focus on one word with one group of children, **or** you may decide to write one key word onto each sheet of paper, and leave all the papers out. The children will then hunt for words to cut out and stick onto the correct piece of paper.

Vocabulary

Any key words that you want to focus on, e.g. the, and, is, on, here

Tip For older children, give each child one piece of paper, for them to collect the complete set of the key words.

Cross-curricular link

PD: Using Equipment and Materials.

Key word race

An energetic running and reading game. Each team has eight key words to read in order to win the game.

Aim

- To develop children's grapheme correspondence so that they can decode words.

Resources

- Set of key words (see vocabulary list opposite)

Preparation

- Enlarge and photocopy the key words onto A4 pieces of card.
- Laminate them to make them more durable if you want to reuse them.
- You will need eight key words for each team (they can be the same eight for each team).

What to do

- Set out the eight key words to make the outline of a square about a metre wide.

Put the children into teams and ask them to line up opposite the square, some distance away.

- The first child runs to the key word square and picks up a word they can read. The child says the word loudly and checks with their team (or an adult) that it's correct.
  They then place the word in the centre of the square before running to the back of his team line.
- The next child runs to the key word square and picks up a card to read. If they read the word wrongly the adult can tell the child what the word says, but the child must then replace the word in its original position in the square before running back to their team.
- Continue until all the words have been read correctly and placed in the centre.
  The first team to read all their words wins the race.

Vocabulary

High-frequency words: see 'Letters and Sounds' in the Appendix.

Tip Choose key words that are becoming familiar to the children.

Cross-curricular link

PD: Movement and Space.

Holidays (2)

Children stick pictures on plates, then use sentence starters to write a holiday diary.

Aim

- To provide an opportunity for children to write simple sentences.

Resources

- Seven paper plates
- Pictures of holiday destinations and houses
- Card for sentences

Preparation

- Prepare some sentence starters: e.g.

  On Monday she went to

  Make one for each day of the week, except Sunday.
  Write: *On Sunday she went home again.*
- Cut out some pictures of tourist destinations. These could be, e.g. a park, the seaside, a forest, a mountain.
- Cut out some pictures of the outsides of houses.

What to do

- Work with a small group of children, and explain that they are going to write a holiday diary for 'Auntie Flo' – or make up your own funny name.
- Let the children choose one house picture and stick it onto a paper plate. This is Auntie Flo's house.
- Look at the destination pictures together and identify them. Each child chooses one place for Auntie Flo to visit on her holiday. They

stick their chosen pictures onto the other paper plates. The plates can now be arranged in a line, finishing with the house.

- Now, show the children the sentence starters. Read them, identifying the days of the week.
  - Can everyone say the days of the week in the right order?
- Place the starter sentences below the paper plates. The first one has the words *On Monday she went to . . . .* The second one has the words *On Tuesday she went to . . .*, and so on until the last one, which will be *On Sunday she went home again*.
- Help the children to write the names for the places she will visit. Place these at the end of the appropriate sentence starter.
  - Can you read her diary?
- Swap the plates around and match the sentences to make a different holiday diary.

Vocabulary

days of the week, diary

Tip Make a collection of books that feature the days of the week in your book corner.

Cross-curricular link

KUW: Time.

Word wall

Use this activity at the start of any new theme or topic. The children make pictures which you label together to create a word bank.

Aim

- To encourage children to use phonic knowledge to read simple words.

Resources

- Available display board and backing paper
- Art materials
- Paper and pens for labels

Preparation

- Cover your display board with a neutral backing paper.

What to do

- Explain to the children about your new theme, e.g. *along our street*.

  What do they think they will be finding out about?
  Make a note of their ideas, e.g. car, bus, market, shop, pelican crossing, traffic lights, people.

- Children can create their own pictures of their ideas with paint, collages or cut-outs from magazines. Let the children help to mount these and attach them to the display.
- Gather the children together near the display board. Point to one of the pictures, and ask the children to tell you what it is.
- Write the word on a large piece of paper. As you write, encourage the children to suggest:
  - what sound it starts with
  - how you will write that down

> - what sound is in the middle
> - what sound comes at the end
> Read the word together when you have finished, and then do the
> same for each picture in turn.
> - When all the words are written, choose a child to come and pick
>   one of the labels and show it to the group.
>   - Who can read it?
>   - Who can point to the picture it matches?
>   Fix the word in place, and continue until your word wall is complete.
> - The children can now use it when they are writing topic-related work.

Vocabulary

Any words linked to your theme

Tip If possible, dedicate one of your display boards for this as a regular starting activity. Attach the pictures and words in a way that allows you to remove them easily so that you can change it regularly.

Cross-curricular link

CD: Being Creative.

Gordon's garage (1)

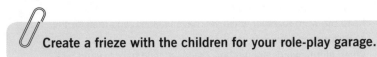

Create a frieze with the children for your role-play garage.

Aim

- To include print in your role-play area for children to read.

Resources

- Pictures of vehicles
- Roll of paper
- Marker pen, glue and scissors

Preparation

- Talk with the children about different kinds of road vehicles: cars, vans, bikes, trucks, etc

    Can they name any specific makes of car?

- Encourage the children to create some pictures of individual vehicles, about A4 size.
- Cut a length of paper from the roll, long enough to form a frieze which you can fix round the inside walls of the role-play area. Lay it along several tables pushed together.

What to do

- Remind the children that they are helping to set up a new role-play area: Gordon's Garage. Tell them,

    'Gordon fixes vehicles in his garage. Which ones might he fix?'

- Let the children show you their pictures, telling everyone what it is, perhaps even the make or model of car.

- Starting at the left-hand side of the paper write, in big bold letters, *Gordon can fix . . . .'*
  - Encourage the children to identify the letters you are writing.
  - Can they guess what the words might say?
  - Read it together when it is done.
- Now choose one of the pictures. The child who made it glues it down onto the frieze, after the words. Underneath write its name/model/make – as the child wishes. Now read the words, *'Gordon can fix a Mini',* for example.
- Add the second picture, and its name, and then read it all again.

  'Gordon can fix a Mini, a bus'
  Continue in this way until you have used all of the pictures.

- Fix your frieze in place around Gordon's Garage.

Vocabulary

car, bike, motorbike, coach, bus, van, lorry, etc.

 Tip Car magazines are a good source of pictures for cutting out if you don't want to spend time making them.

Cross-curricular link

CLL: Role play.

Chapter 6
Enjoying stories and rhymes

Café (2)

> Let the children share the experience of wobbling like Mrs Wobble.

Aim

- To encourage children to compare the feelings of characters with their own experiences.

Resources

- Ahlberg A. (1980) *Mrs Wobble the Waitress*, London: Puffin Books
- Tray
- Unbreakable plates, cups or pans

Preparation

- Share the story with the children up to the part when Mrs Wobble loses her job and all the family are upset.
    - Do the children understand why Mrs Wobble is crying?
    - How do they feel if they see someone crying?
    - Have they ever dropped anything?
    - What was it?
    - What happened?
    - How did they feel?

What to do

- Tell the children that they are going to be waiters/waitresses. Who thinks they can carry a tray of pots?
- Collect together some unbreakable plates, cups or pans. Count them and pile them up on a small tray.
- Let the children take it in turns to walk across the room balancing the pile. Give everyone a clap if they manage to do it.
- If they drop them, everyone shouts '*Mrs Wobble wobbled!*'

Vocabulary

The character names, as well as balance, careful, wobble, drop, tip, fall, how many

Tip To extend the game: let the children estimate how many items they think they'll be able to balance, then encourage them to keep a tally of how many items they carried without wobbling.

Cross-curricular link

PSRN: Numbers as Labels and for Counting.

Who's in the cottage today?

 Children will love this fun way to introduce a story.

Aim

- To provide props to encourage the children to identify the characters in a story.

Resources

- Card for cottage picture (see *Preparation* for details)
- Small pictures of story book characters

Preparation

- Fold a large piece of card so that it will stand up – like a birthday card. On the front, draw and colour a traditional fairy-tale cottage.
- Cut the door on three sides so that it will fold open – like an Advent calendar door.
- Choose one of the character pictures, and fix it in place inside the card so that you can see it when you open the door. Close the door to hide it from view. Fix it so that it can be easily changed for a different character.
- The children might be involved in making the cottage using collage materials, but make the characters yourself so that you don't give the answers away!

What to do

- When the children are sitting ready for their story, show them the cottage. Ask them who might live in a cottage like this one. Encourage as many responses as you can, e.g.
  - Goldilocks
  - one of the Three Bears
  - one of the Three Little Pigs
  - the wolf dressed up as Grandma

- Grandma herself
- Red Riding Hood
- the witch in *Hansel and Gretel*

Why do they think this person might live here? Is there a clue anywhere?

- Now choose a child to come out and open the door to reveal today's character.
  - Did anyone get it right?
  - Can you remind everyone of what happened to that character?
  - Who usually lives in the cottage in this character's story?
- Now tell or read the story to the children.

Tip You might want to extend the idea by having a window that opens, and put another picture clue behind it, to discuss before you open the door.

Cross-curricular link

CD: Developing Imagination and Imaginative Play.

Toot Toot Beep Beep by Emma Garcia (2)

> The children identify the sound words and repeat them at the appropriate places in the story.

Aim

- To help children to match, recognise and read some simple words.

Resources

- A copy of Garcia, E. (2009) *Toot Toot, Beep Beep*, St Albans: Boxer Books
- Pieces of card

Preparation

- Copy one of the sound-effect phrases, e.g. *'vroom vroom'*, onto each card. Make as many copies as you need so that the children can have one each.

What to do

- Introduce the book to the children and then spend some time looking at the first double-spread page. Encourage the children to identify each vehicle by colour and type.
- Look at the second picture of the busy flyover. Which of the vehicles can they see this time?
- As you continue through the book, you read the printed words, and then encourage the children to make the sound-effect noises as you point to the large printed version of the words.
- When you have read and enjoyed the whole story, turn to any page and point to the large print version of the sound effect.

  'Who can remember what this says?'
  'What is the first letter/first sound?'

  Repeat for a few of the other pages.

- Give everyone a card with one sound on it. Ask the children to read them and try to remember what it says. Check that everyone can read their card.
- Now read the story again – without showing the children the pages. At the appropriate places the children should make the sound effect that is written on their card.
- Finish with the page about all the cars being quiet in the car park!

Vocabulary

All the sound effect words in the book

To create a display of colour words:

Tip

- Print on some paper by pressing it into paint that has been spread around with the fingers on a washable surface.
- When dry, cut out shapes to make the vehicles from the story or others of your own design.
- Add your colour names labels.

Cross-curricular link

KUW: Place.

Toot Toot Beep Beep by Emma Garcia (3)

> Write some simple sentences using the ideas in this book and help the children create their own sentences from these ideas.

Aim

- To encourage the children to compose some simple sentences.

Resources

- A copy of Garcia, E. (2009) *Toot Toot Beep Beep*, St Albans: Boxer Books
- Seven strips of card

Preparation

- You will be using the following seven sentences, adapted from the text of the book:

  The red jeep zooms off.
  The black car speeds off.
  The blue van trundles off.
  The yellow taxi rushes off.
  The pink limousine glides off.
  The green camper van rolls off.
  The purple car hurtles off.

  Write five of the sentences onto the strips of card, leaving two strips blank.
- Enjoy the story together before going through the book again, encouraging the children to say some of the words when you pause. Try missing out the colour words and the movement word, e.g.

  'Honk honk goes the . . . . . . city taxi, and off he . . .'

  If necessary, say the first sound of each word to help the children remember.

What to do

- With the children watching, write a sentence on one of the blank strips of card, e.g.

   The yellow taxi rushes off.

   Ask the children if anyone can read this. Let several children have a turn at reading it.
- Now cut the card into three parts,

   The/yellow taxi/rushes off.

   Muddle the pieces up, hand them to three children and ask them if they can put the pieces back together in the correct order. Ask the other children to read and check when they have done this.
- Repeat this process with another sentence.
- Now, read the other sentences with the children.
- Cut all of the strips into three parts, and place the pieces into piles:

   One pile of 'The'
   One pile of vehicle colours and names
   One pile of movements.

- Explain to the children that they should take one card from each pile and use all three pieces to form a sentence.
- Challenge the children to see how many different sentences they can make from these broken sentences.
- Those who are able might choose to copy and illustrate their sentences later.

Vocabulary

sentence, colour words, movement words

Tip
To make an easier version, remove the colour words.
To make a harder version, add the second descriptive word for each vehicle that you will find in the book.

Cross-curricular link

KUW: Place.

Guess the story

> Provide the children with objects and see if they can recognise the story they come from.

Aim

- To encourage the children to recall details from familiar stories.

Resources

- A basket or attractive container
- A selection of story books
- Illustrations of characters and a few objects, e.g.
  - For Cinderella: a party shoe, a mouse, a magic wand
  - For Red Riding Hood: some flowers, a basket, shawl or old-fashioned spectacles
  - For the Three Little Pigs: some straw, a brick, some apples
  - For Goldilocks and the Three Bears: three bowls in different sizes, a broken chair (from the dolls' house), a packet of porridge oats

Preparation

- Choose three books – one that you will read, and any other two.
- Place the objects for the story you will read in your basket, and have your picture of one of the characters ready.

What to do

- When everyone is sitting ready for a story, show the children the basket and identify what is in it.
  - Does this remind the children of any stories that they know?
  - What part do these objects play?
  - Who owns them?
  - If they need a further clue, show them the character's picture.

- Once the children have identified the story, show them the three books.
  - Can they recognise the right one from the cover?
  - Ask the children what clues they can spot on the cover.
- Now read and enjoy your story.

Vocabulary

cover, title, illustration

Variations

Make your clue objects more obscure, e.g. salt and sugar for the Three Bears.

Cross-curricular link

CLL: Story characters.

'Shop, Shop, Shopping' by Georgie Adams

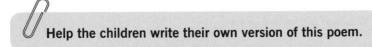

Help the children write their own version of this poem.

Aim

- To provide an opportunity for children to experiment with words and texts.

Resources

- 'Shop, Shop, Shopping' by Georgie Adams can be found in Waters, F. (1999) *Time for a Rhyme*, London: Orion Children's Books.

Preparation

- Read and enjoy the rhyme with the children.
- Can they spot the rhyming words?
- Read it again and see if anyone anticipates the rhymes.

What to do

- Repeat the beginning of the rhyme, then ask the children to help you make a new list of what to buy.

    'What do you buy when you go shopping?'

- When you have a few suggestions, write them down and try to think of words that rhyme.
- Next, choose a rhyming pair and add an adjective to each item, e.g.
    - a red skirt
    - a school shirt
  Continue with two or three more rhyming pairs.
- Finish your poem with the ending of the original poem.

Vocabulary

pairs of rhyming words, e.g.

spoon – balloon
pie – tie
skirt – shirt
fish – dish
peg – egg
jug – mug
map – cap
chocs – box
van – pan
pig – wig

Tip   Next time, try playing this as a remembering game: say the first word and see if the children can provide the rhyme.

Cross·curricular link

KUW: Communities.

Story map

Help a small group of children work together to make a picture of a story.

Aim

- To encourage children to talk about the sequence of events in a story.

Resources

- A large sheet of paper
- Pens and crayons

Preparation

- Read a story of your choice to the children.

What to do

- Arrange a small group of children around the large sheet of paper. Tell them you want to make a big picture of the story.
- Ask who can remember what happens at the beginning of the story. Encourage two children to draw the opening part of the story.
- Then ask what happens next. Encourage the next two children to draw the second part of the story. Continue until the main events in the story have been recorded.
- Now ask the children to retell the story pointing to the pictures they have drawn. As they do this, use a bold felt-tip pen to draw arrows from each picture to the next to indicate the order of events.

- Ask the children if their story map is finished.
  - Can it be improved in any way?
  - How could we show what story it is about?
  - What about adding a title?
  - Does the story map clearly show the order of events?
  - Would it help to add numbers next to the pictures?
- The children may decide they want to add more detail or colour to their pictures.

Vocabulary

beginning, next, ending, order, title, map

 Tip An adult could draw the pictures as very young children retell the events of the story in sequence.

Cross-curricular link

CLL: Story structure.

'Ten Dancing Dinosaurs' by John Foster

Change what happened to the dinosaurs and help the children create a new poem using this classic framework.

Aim

- To provide an opportunity for children to experiment with words and texts.

Resources

- 'Ten Dancing Dinosaurs' can be found in Waters, F. (1999) *Time for a Rhyme*, London: Orion Children's Books.

Preparation

- Read and enjoy the rhyme or choose another one which follows this pattern, e.g. 'Five Little Pussy Cats', found in Matterson, E. (compiler) (1991), *This Little Puffin*, London: Penguin

What to do

- Encourage the children to spot the rhyming words as they listen to the poem.
- Notice that the word at the end of line one rhymes with the number word, e.g.

    'line' – 'nine'.

- Write out the first line of the poem.
- Now suggest to the children that you change what happened to one of the dinosaurs.
- Ask for another idea, e.g.

    One slipped and bumped her head.

- Write the new words but finish the line with the original wording.
- Continue with new ideas about what happened to each dinosaur throughout the poem.

Vocabulary

Lots of interesting vocabulary to discuss in this poem, e.g. *'gyrating'*, *'hijacked'*.

Tip It would be lovely to paint these dancing dinosaurs!

Cross-curricular link

PSRN: Calculating.

Catch That Goat! by Polly Alakija (2)

What happens next? Look for clues in the illustrations as you enjoy this story together.

Aim

- To encourage children to suggest how the story will progress, and end.

Resources

- Alakija, P. (2007) *Catch That Goat!: A Market Day in Nigeria*, Bath: Barefoot Books.

Preparation

- Before you share this story with the children, read the information on the last few pages. This will help you to set the context for children who are not from Nigeria.

What to do

- Each picture in this story book has clues in it as to where the goat or the missing items have gone. Read it slowly, giving the children a chance to look carefully at the illustrations.
  - Who spots the clues?
  - Can they see the goat, or part of the goat?
  - Can they see the missing item?
- Make time to count the items that the market traders have left on their stalls.
- When you reach the page where Mama calls out to Ayoka, stop and ask the children,
  - Can anyone guess where the goat is?
  - Can you guess what the goat has done?
- Encourage the children to work out the ending before you turn to that page.

Tip

This might be an opportunity to look at 'speech bubbles'. Most of the spoken words are in rectangular 'speech bubbles'. Can the children work out why Mama's words at the end of the story are shown in jagged 'bubbles'?

Cross-curricular link

KUW: Communities.

Using finger puppets

Make up a story with the children based on your finger puppet characters.

Aim

- To encourage children to retell narratives in the correct sequence drawing on the language pattern of stories.

Resources

- Animal finger puppets

What to do

- Working with a small group of children, let each child choose an animal finger puppet.
- The adult takes the lead in making up a simple story, encouraging the children to move the puppets and join in or repeat the words, e.g.

> One day a baby elephant was feeling lonely, so he went out for a walk looking for new friends.
> He met a monkey.
> 'Will you play with me?' asked baby elephant.
> 'Not yet,' said monkey. 'I'm looking for nuts.'
> So baby elephant walked on until he met a hippo.
> 'Will you play with me?' asked baby elephant.
> 'Not yet,' said hippo 'I'm rolling in the mud.'
> So baby elephant walked on until he met a penguin . . .

- Continue the narrative with the other animal puppets.

> Until, finally, the last animal said yes!
> Then everyone joined in and played.

Vocabulary

animal names, questions, excuses

Tip This might provide an opportunity to talk with the children about making friends.

Cross-curricular link

PSED: Self-confidence and Self-esteem.

Pants by Giles Andreae and Nick Sharratt

Have fun with this appealing story as the children write about their socks!

Aim

- To help children explore and experiment with sounds, words and texts.

Resources

- Andreae, G. and Sharratt, N. (2002) *Pants*, London: Picture Corgi

Preparation

- Read and enjoy the book with the children.
- Take it in turns to recite the pages using the illustrations to help.

What to do

- Read the first few pages substituting the word '*socks*' for '*pants*'.
- Then ask the children to join in (when they stop laughing!)
- Use the same adjectives and phrasing but change the word '*pants*' for '*socks*' each time as you reread the book together.
- Now ask the children if they can think of other ways to describe socks, e.g.
  - thick socks
  - holey socks
  - smelly socks
  - Christmas socks
  - princess socks
- Try to substitute their suggestions into the rhyme.
- Tell the children you need some different pictures for this new book you've made up.

- Let the children decorate sock shapes with bold patterns. Display them on a washing line with some enlarged words describing the socks.
- More able children could type these out on the computer.

Vocabulary

Adjectives from the book

Tip **When you take down the washing line, staple the socks together and glue in some of the adjectives describing the socks, to make a book for the children to enjoy.**

Cross-curricular link

CD: Being Creative.

Sing along with me

The children record and make their own tapes.

Aim

- To reinforce children's knowledge of rhymes and poems.

Resources

- Cassette player
- Blank tapes – short tapes are more child-friendly

Preparation

- Sing and say rhymes, counting rhymes and short poems together

What to do

- Set up a space where children can come along and record their favourite rhyme.
- Decide how you want to organise these, e.g.
  - One tape for counting rhymes, one for animal rhymes, etc.
  - One tape for one group of children – perhaps an age group or a working group.
- Make sure these are clearly labelled so that the children know which tape to use. An adult can help them so that they understand that they must do their rhyme after the last one already recorded.

  'What will happen if you go over someone else's rhyme?'

- Once completed, each tape can be left out in the music area or the book area for others to enjoy and perhaps join in with.

- Colour code your tapes and leave up a 'key' so that children can be encouraged to choose for themselves.
- You may have the facility to record CDs or use the computer instead.

Tip The children might enjoy creating their own covers for their tapes if you cut the cardboard to fit.

Cross-curricular link

KUW: ICT.

That's When I'm Happy by Beth Shoshan (1)

Act out the events of the story using some simple props to help the children remember.

Aim

- To provide props for children to talk about the sequence of events and characters in a story.

Resources

- Two large teddies and one smaller one
- A copy of Shoshan, B. (2005) *That's When I'm Happy:* London: Little Bee
- A leaf, a star, a small book, a small bed and a small cushion

Preparation

- Read and enjoy the story.
- Ask the children why the small bear might be feeling a little bit sad.

What to do

- Show the children the bears and ask which is which.
- Can they remember two things that Daddy Bear did to cheer up the small bear?
  Show the children the leaf and the star.
- Can they remember two things that Mummy Bear did to cheer up the small bear?
  Show the children the small book and a cushion.
- Can they remember what the small bear did for himself?
  Show the children the small bed.
- Now let the children take turns to retell the story using the props.

Vocabulary

happy, cheerful, sad, sorry, cheer up, smile, remember

Tip   Ask the children about the things that make them happy too.

Cross-curricular link

PSED: Self-care.

That's When I'm Happy by Beth Shoshan (2)

> The children share the experiences described in the story to find their way back to being happy.

Aim

- To encourage children to explore and experiment with texts.

Resources

- A copy of Shoshan, B. (2005) *That's When I'm Happy*: London: Little Bee
- Leaves, sticky stars, large piece of dark coloured paper, cushions and books

Preparation

- Read and enjoy the story.
- Talk about the central theme of getting back to feeing happy when you feel a bit sad.

What to do

- Tell the children you are going to try out the ideas in the story. After each experience, encourage them to talk about how they are feeling.
- Go outside and kick through the leaves. Choose a special one to show everyone. Collect some in a bag to bring inside to make a collage.
- Sit on some cushions with a friend. Choose a favourite book from the book corner to read with a friend. Can you find a word that begins with the same letter as your name?
- Let the children stick hundreds of stars all over a big piece of black paper.
  Count to a hundred together.
- Everyone lies down on the floor and goes to sleep!

- Do they think the ideas are successful for getting back to being happy?
- Let the children vote for the best way of cheering up, and record their findings, e.g.
    - everyone has a smiley face to stick on the sheets labelled with the various activities or
    - use a computer program that allows you to record information as a graph
- What other ideas would they suggest?

Vocabulary

laugh, smile, giggle, happy

Tip To do this with a large group, set out all the activities, then sets of children can move between them with a supporting adult and report back.

Cross-curricular link

PSED: Making Relationships.

Good Morning Mrs Hen

> Change the colour words in this rhyme to create your own rainbow of chicks with the children.

Aim

- To help children understand what a word is.

Resources

- A copy of *Good Morning Mrs Hen* can be downloaded from http://www.bigeyedowl.co.uk/show_songs.php?t=1

Preparation

- Make an enlarged copy of the poem.
- Two pieces of card that can be stuck over words on the poem with reusable adhesive.

What to do

- Read and learn the poem with the children. Point to the words as you read together, encouraging them to recognise the words.
- Highlight the colour words – yellow, brown and red.
- Explain that these words are the colours of hens and chicks, but you are going to have fun pretending they are other colours.
- Tell the children that they can change two colour words.
- Ask the children who can point to the words 'yellow' and 'red'? Cover these words with small pieces of card.
- Read the poem again, pausing at the blanked-out word. Ask for suggestions of other colours and write these on your cards. Now, reread your poem, e.g.

    four of them are pink

- Repeat the activity with different colours to create lots of new rhymes.

Vocabulary

yellow, brown, red, pink, green, orange, blue, turquoise, purple, black, white

Tip Draw and cut out ten chicks and arrange them into different groups to make ten, e.g. seven in one group and three in another, or one group of two, one of three and another of five.

Cross-curricular link

PSRN: Calculating.

Tiddalick by Robert Roennfeldt (1)

Children act out the events in this traditional story from Australia.

Aim

- To help children start to recognise how stories can be structured.

Resources

- Roennfeldt, R. (1980) *Tiddalick, the Frog Who Caused a Flood,* London: Picture Puffins

Preparation

- In this traditional tale, based on an Aboriginal Dreamtime legend, the structure is:
  - There is a problem.
  - Different strategies to solve it are tried.
  - Eventually one of them works and there is a successful outcome.
- Look at the title page to see all the animals that appear in the story. Help the children to remember their names.
- Share the story with the children.

What to do

- Think about each character in the story in turn and what they say or do:
  - Everyone can try being a small frog, and then slowly getting bigger and bigger, and then quickly shrinking back to their normal size.
  - Everyone can pretend to tell a very funny story. Choose a simple joke that the children can tell, and they can laugh as they tell it.
  - Playing leapfrog would not be appropriate – so either use two stuffed animals to do this, or everyone can do 'bunny jumps'.

- Strut around like the lizard with tummies puffed out.
- Everyone can dance like the eel.
- Now read the story again, with the children acting out all the parts as they occur.
- The children could now work in small groups to retell the story themselves – without you reading the book for them. The order of the animals' efforts doesn't matter as long as the eel is last.

Vocabulary

the characters' names
'Once, long ago . . . .' or 'Once upon a time …' – useful story opener.

Tip

'**Dreamtime' is an Aboriginal concept of the creation of the world and includes many stories, some of which explain how people should behave. You can find out more about this if you do an Internet search for 'Aboriginal Dreamtime'.**

Tiddalick **would be a useful book to link with the idea of sharing, and of the effects of being greedy.**

Cross-curricular link

PSED: Making Relationships.

Tiddalick by Robert Roennfeldt (2)

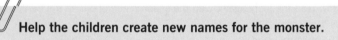

Help the children create new names for the monster.

Aim

- To encourage the children to explore and experiment with sounds, words and texts.

Resources

- A copy of Roennfeldt, R. (1981) *Tiddalick: The Frog Who Caused a Flood*, London: Picture Puffins
- A soft toy version or puppet of the character if available

Preparation

- Read and enjoy the story.
- Discuss the character: how he looks and how he behaves in the story.

What to do

- Sit together in a circle. Ask the children who can remember the monster's name. Take turns saying his name in 'monstery' voices.
- *Why do you think Tiddalick was called that?* If the children suggest something to do with licking, for example, use this idea to suggest a different name such as Licklack or Biggerlick.
- When the children have stopped laughing, ask them if they can think of another name for him. Praise everyone's attempts.
- If you have a puppet or soft toy, make it nod enthusiastically at everyone's ideas.

Tip   Don't try to write the new names down!

Cross-curricular link

CD: Being Creative.

Jack and Jill

Act out the events in sequence to illustrate the beginning, middle and end of a familiar rhyme.

Aim

- To help the children to understand the elements of a story.

Preparation

- Make sure the children are all familiar with the rhyme and can repeat it from memory.

What to do

- Say the rhyme together.
- Ask the children if they can tell you what is happening at the beginning of the rhyme.

    'Jack and Jill are going up a hill'.

- Choose two children to act this out.
- Ask the children if they know what happened next.

    'Jack fell down. Then Jill fell down the hill.'

- Choose some more children to act this out.
- And how does it all end?

    'Jack gets up and goes home.'

- Another group of children act this out.
- What do they think happened to Jill?
- Now position three groups of 'actors', one set for each part – the beginning, the middle and the end. These children can mime appropriate actions at the right time, as the other children repeat the rhyme.

Vocabulary

beginning, middle, end

> You could try this with other rhymes where the three elements can be easily identified, e.g.
>
> Pat-a-cake, pat-a-cake, baker's man
>
> Two little dicky-birds
>
> Incy Wincy Spider

Tip

Cross-curricular link

CLL: Story structure.

Bigger and bigger (1)

Help the children to read and interpret the repeated phrases in a familiar picture book.

Aim

- To develop children's understanding of the language of stories and how print works.

Resources

- A copy of Rosen, M. (1993) *We're Going on a Bear Hunt,* London: Walker Books
- Other books that have repeated phrases where the print is gradually enlarged

What to do

- When the children have enjoyed the story a few times, look at one of the pages that describes the character's movement e.g.

  'Stumble trip, stumble trip, stumble trip'

- Can the children see that the words are repeated three times? Help them count.
- Ask if they notice anything that is different as the words are repeated on the page. Show them how the words get bigger and bigger and bigger.
  - Why do you think the words are printed like that?
- Listen to the children's suggestions and try out their ideas, e.g. they may suggest the words could be said slower and slower because they were feeling tired, or quicker and quicker as they went faster.
- Try reading the words quietly the first time, then louder and louder to illustrate one idea.

- Read the book again and encourage the children to join in the repeated phrases, starting with a whisper and ending with a shout!
- Ask the children to find other books that enlarge print in this way.
- Leave out a few examples for the children to explore.

Vocabulary

small, large, larger, quiet, loud, louder

Tip For more ideas using this wonderful book see *Games, Ideas and Activities for Early Years Phonics* in the Classroom Gems series.

Cross-curricular link

PSRN: Shape, Space and Measures.

Bigger and bigger (2)

The children create their own repeated phrases and enlarge the font using a computer.

Aim

- To develop children's understanding of the language of stories and how print works.

Resources

- Books that have repeated phrases where the print is gradually enlarged
- Writing program on the computer

Preparation

- To help the children understand the convention of enlarging print, read several books that demonstrate this or use activity 'Bigger and bigger (1)', p. 224.

What to do

- When the children have enjoyed the chosen story a few times, look at one of the pages that illustrate print getting larger.
- Talk about how this makes the story more exciting, e.g. *'It helps us know the beanstalk is growing higher and higher.'*
- Think of other story situations when words might be repeated, e.g.
  – A monster coming nearer and nearer
- Let the children choose a starting word and type it on the computer (see vocabulary list below). Show them how to add *–er* to the ending of their word.
- Help them to type or copy the new word three times.
- Then show them how to change the size of the font and make it larger.
- Let the children experiment until they choose the best size.
- Print out their repeating phrases and display them for others to read.

Vocabulary

small – smaller
large – larger
quiet – quieter
loud – louder
high – higher
near – nearer

Tip Explain that the word still needs to fit on the paper when you print it if someone is getting carried away with font enlargement!

Cross·curricular link

KUW: ICT.

Bigger and bigger (3)

Use the children's own ideas for repeated phrases to create music that grows louder or quieter.

Aim

- To develop children's understanding of the language of stories and how print works.

Resources

- Percussion instruments
- Writing program on the computer

Preparation

- Use activity 'Bigger and bigger (2)', p, 226, to introduce the idea of print being enlarged.

What to do

- Play one of the instruments. Ask the children to think of a word to describe the sound, e.g. *bang* or *crash*
- Write the word three times, once in small print, then larger and larger. Demonstrate how to play the instrument by getting louder or quieter as indicated by the size of the print on the repeated words.
- Let the children work in pairs and select an instrument.
- Now ask them to think of a word to describe the sound of their instrument.
- Help the children write their words on a computer writing program.
- Ask them to copy their word three times. Then change the size of their word so that it gets bigger and bigger.
- Print out the children's words.

- Now one child points at the repeated words in three sizes of print while their partner plays the instrument matching the volume to the size of the print.
- Let the children take it in turns to play or point.
- The children can then try playing another set of words on a different instrument.
- When they are confident with the idea that small print = quiet, an adult can conduct a group of children playing a range of instruments using the words:

> play, play, play

Have fun!

Vocabulary

bang, crash, boom, ting, ring, click, shake, rattle, squeak, toot

Tip Perhaps you could introduce the children to the musical symbol for a crescendo.

Cross-curricular link

CD: Creating Music and Dance.

Part 3
Writing

Allow children to see adults reading and writing and encourage children to experiment with writing for themselves through making marks, personal writing symbols and conventional script.

Practice Guidance for the Early Years Foundation Stage, May 2008, p. 42

Chapter 7
Finger play

Candles (4)

The children enjoy using finger painting to create their own candle designs.

Aim

- To encourage children to make shapes of letters in their play.

Resources

- Finger paint in bright colours
- Large sheets of paper

Preparation

- Fill in a candle-shape of paint on a table.
- Cut out paper that is larger than this.

What to do

- Encourage the children to use their fingertip to make a design in the paint. Try:
  - circles
  - long and short straight lines
  - zig-zags

oooo

lili

ww

These are the basic shapes that we use to write our letters.
- Now lay the paper carefully on top of the paint.
- Press gently and then remove to reveal your candle.
- The children can now add a yellow 'flame' to their candle, using paint and a brush, or a shape cut from yellow paper.

Vocabulary

round, straight, joined

Tip Some children might like to prepare their own candle shapes on the table.

Cross-curricular link

CD: Exploring Media and Materials.

Keep those fingers moving

> Try warming up the finger muscles with some simple fun exercises before the children start their handwriting,

Aim

- To encourage the children to practise manipulative skills ready for writing.

Resources

- A good supply of action rhymes

What to do

- Just as an athlete warms up his muscles before a competition, it is worth doing some finger exercises before children are expected to practise their handwriting skills. Any action rhyme that involves finger movements can be used, e.g.

    Two Little Dicky Birds
    Tommy Thumb
    Five Little Men in a Flying Saucer

- Or create your own set of exercises. Here are two ideas to start with:
  - Spread your hand out on the table, palm down.

      Who can lift each finger in turn without their other fingers moving?
      How fast can you do it?
      How slowly can you do it?
      Are you quicker than your friend?

  - Can your thumb touch each of your fingers, one after the other? It must be the fingers on the same hand as the chosen thumb!

      Can you do it with your other hand?
      How fast can you do it?

Vocabulary

thumb, finger, wiggle, stretch, curl

Tip Children may soon be able to do some of these independently when you ask them to warm up their fingers ready for writing.

Cross-curricular link

PD: Using Equipment and Materials.

Ribbon dance

 The children swirl their ribbons around as they dance.

Aims

- To provide opportunities for the children to use large shoulder movements.

Resources

- Long lengths of ribbon
- Recorded music

Preparation

- Record some music which is lively, but with an even tempo. Waltz music is a good range to try.
- Talk with the children about the dancers in a carnival parade and how they might be waving ribbons, and making patterns with them in the air.

What to do

- The children can spend some time dancing freely to the music, swirling their ribbons high in the air, to practise the movement.
- Once they are familiar with how to make their ribbon 'dance', ask them to follow you all over the area. Explain to them that they will be like dancers in a carnival parade.
- Ask the children to try to make their ribbons move in a circle in the air. Encourage all of them to make their ribbons go in the same direction.
- Explain that when you give them a signal, they should change the direction that their ribbon is going in, making a circle the other way. Show them the signal. You might raise one hand or the other, or blow a whistle.

- When everyone needs to sit down and have a rest, ask the children:

    'Is it easier with one of your hands?'
    'Which one?'
    'Is it the same hand that you use when you write or draw?'

- On another occasion, try making zig-zag shapes.

Vocabulary

left, right, high, low

 Tip The leader could carry a baton, flag or flower to use as an indicator of where the parade is going, or which way to twirl your ribbon.

Cross·curricular link

KUW: Communities.

Stripy flags

A chance for children to practise their hand control as they use a computer mouse to make flags.

Aim

- To provide an opportunity to manipulate objects with increasing control.

Resources

- Computer with mouse
- Simple art program e.g. First Paint

Preparation

- Show the children how to click on the colours they want to use.
- Give the children opportunities to play, making marks freely using different colours.

What to do

- Tell the children that they are going to make some flags.
- Demonstrate how to use the computer program:
  - Select the widest paintbrush symbol on the computer program.
  - Remind the children how to select the colour they want to choose.
  - Use the mouse to draw a wobbly horizontal line across the top of the screen.
  - Then select a second colour and draw a similar line under the first.
  - Continue the process by selecting and drawing lines with a third and fourth colour.
- Print out your design and show the children your flag.
- The children can now have a turn at making their own flags.
- As the children produce their flags, fix them to a line hanging over the classroom door or across a display board.

Vocabulary

click, press, hold, across, under

Tip　Encourage the children to work slowly in order to control their stripes.

Cross-curricular link

KUW: ICT.

Birthday (4)

> Celebrate with an iced cake, and make it into an opportunity for the children to practise writing their letters.

Aim

- To give children practise in forming letters correctly.

Resources

- Ready-made or pre-prepared cake or cakes
- Icing sugar and water mixed
- Food colouring and cocktail sticks (with points cut off) or icing pens

Preparation

- Choose which type of cake you want to decorate with the children:
  - A ready-made cake large enough for one name
  - Ready-made small cakes
- Choose either to use icing tubes or to let the children use a clean cocktail stick dipped in food colouring to write in the icing while it is still damp.
- Let the children help you ice the cake/s with a layer of water icing.

What to do

- Show the children the cakes and explain that you are going to decorate them with letters.
- Demonstrate how to write with the icing, reminding the children of the correct letter formation.
- Help the children as they decorate the cake/s with written icing.
- If you are using small cakes, try one of these ideas:
  - The children have a cake each and write the first letter of their own name on it.
  - Each child can write one letter on their cake so that altogether they spell out 'happy birthday' or a toy's name. Can they arrange them to spell out the words?

- If you decide to use a large cake, let the children take turns writing letters on the cake to make the toy's name or 'happy birthday'.

Vocabulary

start, top, down, over, round, up, squeeze

Tip Practise your icing writing on greaseproof paper first.

Cross-curricular link

PSED: Sense of Community.

Musical marks (1)

Children enjoy moving to some soothing music and then paint as they listen again.

Aim

- To encourage children to use their hands to make left-to-right movements.

Resources

- Soothing music e.g. Dvorak's *New World Symphony*.
- Large pieces of paper, paint and brushes.

Preparation

- Prepare the paper and paint on covered surfaces.

What to do

- Play the music to the children.
- Encourage them to move with the music in appropriate ways, e.g. flowing arm movements and turning slowly
- Explain to the children that you are going to play the music again, but this time they are going to paint as they listen.
- Play the music and encourage the children to paint long, smooth waves of colour across the paper. Encourage them to start at the left and finish on the right.
- When the paint is dry discuss what it looks like, e.g.

    blue paint – water/sea/sky
    green paint – grass/hills
    orange/red – sunset

Vocabulary

smooth, long, gently, slow, flowing, rising and falling

Tip Use these paintings as a background and let the children add details like boats, flowers, sheep, etc. to fit the theme of the background colour.

Cross-curricular link

CD: Being Creative.

Musical marks (2)

Children have fun making quick flicking movements as they listen to fast, exciting music.

Aim

- To encourage children to use their fingers to make shapes in the air and to make marks.

Resources

- Strong quick music, e.g. Rimsky-Korsakov: *Flight of the Bumble Bee*.
- Large pieces of paper, broad felt-tip pens.

Preparation

- Prepare the paper on covered surfaces.

What to do

- Play the music to the children. Encourage them to move with the music in appropriate ways, e.g. fast, flicking movements with their fingers, arms and legs.
- Explain to the children that you are going to play the music again, as they paint. Encourage them to draw quick flicking marks on the paper. Allow them to do this freely at random on the paper using a range of bright colours.
- Or, provide a circle template in the centre of the paper that can be removed later to reveal a sunburst.

- Show the children how to start on the card circle and then make flicks off the edges of the circle onto the paper.

Vocabulary

quick, flick, spiky, short, sharp, fast, jerky

Tip Try it again using chalk on dark paper to create a fireworks picture.

Cross-curricular links

CD: Being Creative.

Paper play

> The children create a display by tearing paper. This strengthens the fine muscles in their hands and fingers.

Aim

- To encourage the children to practise manipulative skills.

Resources

- Backing paper and glue
- Picture 1: Sugar paper in shades of green and brown
- Picture 2: Newspapers

Preparation

- Cut out a piece of paper large enough to cover one of your display boards.

What to do

Picture 1:

- Explain to the children that they are going to create a forest on the display board.
- Show them how to make some trees from the sugar paper by tearing the paper. Explain how tearing will give a jagged edge to the shapes which will look more lifelike. Children can now tear the green shades of paper into large 'cloud' shapes for the tops of the trees. They will also need to tear the brown shades into long strips to make the tree trunks.
- Help them to glue these onto the backing paper to look like a forest.
- Children can add cut-out painted figures of children on a walk, or animals that live in a wood, or Hansel, Gretel and the witch's cottage – anything that will suit your current theme of work.

Picture 2:

- Explain to the children that they are going to create a display about a busy town, using only old newspapers. Discuss what might be in a town, e.g. buildings, traffic, roads. Mark a road across the lower part of your display board with a black marker pen.
- The children tear out rectangular shapes from the sheets of newsprint in a variety of sizes.
- Help them to stick the larger shapes onto the backing paper to look like a townscape of buildings. Use smaller rectangles to represent cars, buses, etc.
- When the glue is dry, help the children to draw wheels and windows onto the newsprint shapes with black felt-tip pens.

Vocabulary

tear, torn, rip

Tip Tearing strengthens the same muscles that you need for controlling a pencil.

Cross-curricular link

PD: Using Equipment and Materials.

Letter shapes

Turn handwriting practice into an art activity for the children.

Aim

- To encourage children to practise forming letter shapes.

Resources

- Marker pens
- *Picture 1*: Light brown, green or pink paper
- *Picture 2*: Pink or light brown paper

Preparation

- *Picture 1*: Cut the paper into roof shapes. Try to make a variety of shapes.
- *Picture 2*: Cut the paper into rectangles.
- Put a small mark in the top left-hand corner of each paper so that children know where to start.

What to do

Picture 1:

- Explain to the children that they are going to add some 'tiles' onto the roof-shaped pieces of paper. Start by making one yourself as the children watch you so that they can work out what you want them to do.
- Show the children how to make a row of 'u' shapes, joined together, along the top of the roof shape, working from left to right. Remind them that they should start where you have marked the dot.
- Now, make some more rows, one under the other. When the shape is full of letter 'u's the design should look like roof tiles.
- Now let children choose one of the roof shapes and a colourful felt-tip pen. Encourage them to take care, but to keep their pen moving across the roof.
- Children can make as many as they want. Have plenty of shapes available in case anyone needs to start again.

- When all the shapes are completed, the children can help to stick the rooftops onto the lower half of some dark backing paper. Add chimneys, stars, some snow and a Father Christmas figure to complete your winter's night scene.

Picture 2:

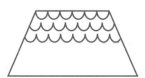 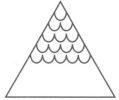

- Explain to them that they can make a picture of a crowd of people.
- Demonstrate the process as for Picture 1, so that the children can imagine the finished image.
- Give each child a sheet of pink or light brown paper.
- Encourage them to use their pens to make circles, across the page, moving from left to right. They can make as many rows as they can fit onto their paper.
- When the paper is full the children can add eyes, mouths and a little hair to make funny faces as they create their own crowd of people.

Vocabulary

left, right, up, down, over, round

Tip   Encourage left to right movements, and moving from top to bottom of the paper.

Cross-curricular link

PD: Using Equipment and Materials.

Mini-beasts (4)

Children use silver pens to make their own snail trail as they practise working from left to right across the page.

Aim

- To encourage children to manipulate objects with increasing control.

Resources

- Snails – if possible
- Silver marker pens
- Dark-coloured sugar paper
- Circles of paper in a contrasting colour

Preparation

- Have some garden snails for children to observe.
- Let the children watch them move across dark-coloured paper towards some tempting pieces of cucumber. Point out their trails.

What to do

- Explain to the children that they are going to make their own snail trails. They will use their silver marker pen to make a trail.
  - Can they think why the pens are this colour?
  - Do they remember what the real snail trail looked like?
- Remind the children to start at the left side of the paper and make a trail over to the right. They can try to make some looped lines or curves as part of their preparation for writing.
- When they have completed their silver trail, the children can stick a paper circle at the right-hand end of the line.

- When it is dry they can try to draw a spiral shape on the circle with brightly coloured pens.
- Add features to complete your snail, and maybe draw a piece of cucumber for him!

Vocabulary

round, across, left, right, loop, spiral

 Tip Use your snail trail to suggest some phonics work on rhyming strings of words, e.g. 'a pale whale snail trail'.

Cross-curricular link

KUW: Exploration and Investigation.

Write outside

A selection of ideas for ways that the children can practise their writing outdoors.

Aim

- To provide the children with a variety of writing tools.

Resources

- Chalk
- Empty washing-up bottles
- Sticks, pebbles, leaves or cones

Preparation

- Collect together the outdoor writing tools you want to use today.
- Before going outside:
  - Make sure everyone is dressed appropriately – some may need aprons on.
  - Explain why natural materials are good for writing outdoors.
  - Help them understand that they can only write in the areas you show them, and with the tools you have given them.

What to do

- Explain to the children that they are going to write outside today.
- Remind the children of a word (e.g. their name) or letter shape you want them to practise.
- Before you go outside remind them to start at the left side.
  - Can everybody remember which side that is?
  Practise the writing pattern in the air.

- When you get outside, demonstrate how and where each tool may be used:
  - Chalk or squirty water bottles are for writing on hard surfaces.
  - Use blunt sticks to write in the sandpit.
  - The pebbles, cones and leaves can be placed on the grass to form letter shapes.

Vocabulary

left, right, top, down, up, round, over

Tip This activity (as with most writing activities) should be well supervised if good writing habits are to be encouraged.

Cross-curricular link

PD: Using Equipment and Materials.

Jolly jigsaw

> Children draw a picture and then cut it up to make their own jigsaw.

Aim

- To encourage the children to use fine motor control skills.

Resources

- Large pieces of card in pale colours
- Children's broad felt-tip pens and scissors
- Pencil and ruler for the adult

Preparation

- Experience of playing with jigsaws.

What to do

- Talk to the children about the jigsaws in your setting.
  - Which is their favourite?
  - Which one is the hardest?
- Tell them they are going to make their own jigsaw.
- Ask everyone to make a colourful pattern or picture on a piece of card. Encourage them to fill all the available space and ask them to use every colour in the box! When their picture is finished remind them to write their name on it.
- Then turn the card over and let the child watch as you draw four or five interlocking lines across the reverse of the card using a pencil and ruler.

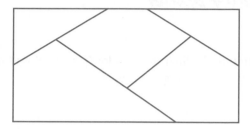

The child now draws along the lines with a felt-tip pen before you help them cut carefully along the lines with the scissors.

- Now they can have a go at remaking the jigsaw, then share it with another child.

Vocabulary

straight, line, scissors, cut

Tip This activity can be varied to suit the ability of the children, e.g. jigsaws with only three or four pieces will be suitable for very young children.

Cross-curricular link

CD: Exploring Media and Materials.

Incy Wincy Spider

Children make their own spider from wool and pipe cleaners before sharing the rhyme.

Aim

- To encourage the children to use fine motor skills.

Resources

- Pipe cleaners
- Wool
- Sequins
- Scissors and glue

Preparation

- Make sure everyone knows the rhyme, *Incy Wincy Spider*.
- Talk about real spiders:
  - Who has seen a spider?
  - What do they look like?
  - How do they move?
  - What size are they?
  - How many legs do they have?

What to do

- Tell the children they are going to make their own spider.
- Help each child count out four pipe cleaners to use.
- Now show them how to wrap the wool around the centre of the bundle of four pipe cleaners. They should keep winding until the wool creates a body for the spider. Then help the children cut the wool with the scissors but remember to leave a long length of wool so the spider can dangle down. An adult can make a knot so the wool can't unwind.

- Now let the children choose two matching sequins to create eyes for their spider.
- Help them glue the eyes onto the spider's body.
- Let the children move their spider as they recite the rhyme.
- Write out the rhyme in large print and dangle the spiders around it to create a display.

Vocabulary

numbers 1–4, wind, wool, scissors, cut, sequins, dangle

Tip If you want to extend this into a writing activity – write out the instructions for making the spider on separate strips of paper and ask the children to arrange them in the correct order.

Cross·curricular link

PD: Using Equipment and Materials.

Café (3)

> A fun opportunity for writing as the children create some menus.

Aims

- To encourage children to use their ability to hear the sounds at the beginning of words.

Resources

- Printed pictures or drawings of food
- Pieces of A4 card folded in half
- Glue, felt-tip pens
- Ahlberg A. (1980) *Mrs Wobble the Waitress*, London: Puffin Books

Preparation

- After reading the story, focus on the page where Mr Wobble and the children make menus.
- Decide with the children six to eight items of food to sell in their café.
- An adult prints out multiple clip art pictures of these items (or photocopies simple drawings).

What to do

- Show the children the folded pieces of card that will become the menus.
- Discuss the way the menu in *Mrs Wobble the Waitress* is organised with pictures and writing side by side.
- Lay out the pictures of the food, and encourage the children to identify the items.
- Let each child choose the ones for their own menu.
- Help the children glue the pictures into the menus, leaving spaces for their writing.
- Encourage them to make an attempt to write the words next to the appropriate pictures.

Vocabulary

Various food items, e.g. tea, milkshake, coke, juice, soup, burger, sandwich, fruit, ice cream

Tip Choosing words that each have a different initial letter will be helpful to children who are beginning to make use of phonic knowledge as they attempt to write words

Cross-curricular link

PD: Health and Bodily Awareness.

Chapter 8
Writing it down

Cinderella's busy day

Start by playing a memory game with the children and then they write a list of jobs for Cinderella to do.

Aim

- To encourage the children to attempt writing in the form of a list.

Resources

- Strips of card and felt-tip pens
- Magnetic board and magnets
- Pre-prepared paper for lists

Preparation

- For the role play: print some long lengths of paper, like a shopping list notepad.
  - At the top put, '*Cinderella, today you must . . .*'
  - At the bottom put, '*Signed . . . .*'
  - In between, list the numbers 1, 2 and 3 well spaced out.

What to do

- Sit in a circle with a small group of children to play a game. Explain to them that they are pretending to be the Ugly Sisters. Remind them how they were always spiteful to Cinderella, expecting her to do everything for them.
- You start the game by saying '*This morning I want Cinderella to . . . . . .*' and add a chore for her to do.
- Each child in turn repeats what has gone before and adds one more job to the list. You may need to limit this to four or five suggestions.

- As each chore is mentioned an adult can quickly write it down on individual strips of card. Stick these up as a list as they are given. You could use, e.g.
  - sweep the floor
  - polish the table
  - wash the dishes
  - light the fire
  - feed the cat
  - wash my dress
  - peel the potatoes
  - butter the bread
  - do the shopping
  - clean my shoes

  Children can use the list to remind them of what has already been said.
- Now, take down the list and then play again. Children might use the same ideas but in a different order, or you might have to write out new ideas that they have thought of. Create the new list accordingly.
- Show the children the prepared paper for writing their own lists. Read it with them.
- Explain to them that when they are playing in the role-play area they can make a list of chores for Cinderella to do and fix it up on the magnetic board. The list you created during your game can be displayed nearby in case some children would like to use these ideas.

Tip If you are the only adult with the group, write down your opening chore before you start the game, to speed up the process.

Cross-curricular link

CLL: Role play.

What's in your box?

If you are preparing boxes of fruit as gifts for the members of your community at harvest time, help the children to record the contents using this simple sentence structure.

Aim

- To help the children form simple sentences.

Resources

- Strips of paper
- Pictures of fruits with labels
- Small boxes

Preparation

- Each child will need two strips of paper, one with '*I have*' written on it, and one with '*in my box*.' Don't forget to include the full stop.
- Collect pictures of fruits. Stick them onto individual cards with the name written on the reverse. Include 'a' or 'an' or 'some' as appropriate, e.g. '*a pear*', '*an apple*', '*some grapes*'.

What to do

- Model this activity with the group of children, before expecting them to work on their own version.
- Place one of your '*I have*' cards in front of you. Now choose a picture card and place it next. After this place an '*in my box*.' strip of paper.
- Read out the sentence, including the name of the fruit, drawing children's attention to the capital letter at the beginning of the sentence and the full stop at the end.

- The children can now have a go at writing this. Give each child their own sentence opening and closing words. They can choose to draw a picture or write the name of the fruit as part of their sentence.
- Children can make as many sentences as they wish and then illustrate their work with a box of fruit, but . . . .
  . . . make sure it matches the words!

Vocabulary

sentence, full stop, capital letter

Tip Your able children might like to try inserting a colour word before the name of the fruit, e.g. '*I have a yellow banana.*' '*I have some green grapes.*'

Cross-curricular link

PSED: Sense of Community.

Dear Bear

Write a letter from a teddy bear for your children to read. Use this opportunity to develop their understanding of another country.

Aim

- To provide a reason for your children to use writing in their play.

Resources

- A new teddy bear or similar soft toy
- Paper, pens and pencils

Preparation

- The adult writes a letter as if it is from the bear and leaves it for the children to find in the classroom.
- The bear tells the children he is coming from another country to visit them.
- Try to ask a simple question in the letter e.g. Can you guess where I live?

What to do

- Once the children have found the letter, help them read what it says. Show them the paper and pens and encourage them to write a reply. Allow the children to write freely in their own way.
- Next day the bear writes back telling them something about his country and then asks them to guess what he can see from his window.
- Continue the letter exchange for as long as the children are keen, asking questions such as: What is my job? Can you guess what I wear? Then ask a final question, e.g. How will I find your school?
- Arrange a day when the new bear will visit. Discuss how to make their new friend welcome – perhaps have a little tea party when the new bear comes.

Vocabulary

This will vary depending on the country you choose, e.g.
>Australia: beach, surf, sunshine, suncream, barbecue, lifeguard
>Norway: mountain, high, climb, fjord, boat, fisherman, mountain rescue

 Tip Don't forget, children can draw pictures as their way of communicating.

Cross-curricular link

KUW: Communities.

Wedding (2)

Write name labels with the children and use them to create a seating plan as if they were guests at a wedding.

Aim

- To support children in recognising and writing their own names.

Resources

- Card and pens
- Two or three small tables and chairs

Preparation

- Help the children to write their names on pieces of card.
- Show them the name cards and help the children recognise theirs.

What to do

- Tell the children that after a wedding everyone usually shares a meal together.
  Explain that the bride and groom plan where the guests will sit – called a seating plan – and that name cards will mark everyone's place at the table.
- Choose two of your names for the bride and groom. Let one child put these name cards in place.
- Now explain that the bride wants every girl to sit next to a boy. Help the other children to put names on the table in this way.
- Read the names with the children to check that the positioning is correct. All the children can now find their names and sit down. Talk about who is sitting next to who.
- Remove the name cards and play again with a different seating arrangement, e.g. all boys on one table and all girls on another.

Vocabulary

name, next to, who?, where?

 Tip More able children can use a simple, drawn seating plan to position the name cards on the tables.

Cross-curricular links

PSED: Sense of Community.

Holidays (3)

Help the children make a postcard by sticking a holiday picture on one side, then writing a message on the other.

Aim

- To provide an opportunity for children to do some independent writing.

Resources

- Blank postcards or pieces of card
- Holiday brochures

Preparation

- Send a postcard to school from a holiday destination you have visited.
- Read the postcard to the children.
- Explain that the photograph shows the place you were visiting.

What to do

- Ask the children if they have been on holiday.
  - Where did they go?
- Show the children the holiday brochures and talk about the different types of places, e.g. seaside, theme park.
- Let the children cut out their favourite picture.
- Show them how to stick it on one side of the card to make a postcard. Discuss who to send it to.
- Now let the children write a message on the back of the postcard. Talk about what to write, e.g. 'We went for a swim.'
  Remind them how to finish their message with their own name.
- Show the children where to write their parent or friend's name.
- Display these by hanging them from lengths of string so that both sides can be admired.

Vocabulary

seaside, hotel, pool, villa, theme park, funfair, holiday village, mountains, lakes

Tip To keep this activity simple we don't suggest addressing the postcards, although this may be something you could include with your older children.

Cross-curricular link

KUW: Place.

On the climbing frame

Enjoy some outdoor writing fun. Help the children use split sentences to describe their positions on the climbing frame.

Aim

- To encourage children to reread their writing as they write.

Resources

- Felt-tip pens and paper
- Sentences written on strips of card

Preparation

- Write some simple sentences on strips of card describing positions on and around your climbing frame, e.g.
  - I am on / the rope
  - I am under / the slide
  - I am near / the logs
- Cut the strips into two pieces, as indicated, so the children can rearrange them to create a variety of sentences.

What to do

- Explain to the children that they are going to play on the climbing frame, but that you will stop them every now and again and ask them to tell you where they are.
  By doing this the children will have spoken many of the words written on your cards.
- Now, collect the children together and read the sentences you prepared. Show the children how they can swap the sentence parts to create new sentences.

- Let the children choose which sentence they would like to write, using the beginnings and ends of the sentences.
- Encourage everyone to read the sentence they have written. Now they can go and take up that position on the climbing frame.
- Allow another session of free play on the climbing equipment, then call the children together again to create a different sentence with another beginning and end from the split sentences.
- Read their sentence and again find the position on the climbing frame.

Vocabulary

on, under, near, behind, in front, high, low, next to

Tip Create a small drawing of your climbing frame and photocopy it so the children can draw the position that they wrote about.

Cross-curricular link

PSRN: Shape, Space and Measures.

Ten Fat Sausages

Use this familiar rhyme to inspire the children to write *Pop* or *Bang*. Then use their writing as you recite the rhyme together.

Aim

- To encourage children to write simple words.

Resources

- Ten sheets of A4 paper

Preparation

- Cut five pieces of paper into circles and five into 'explosions' (jagged shapes).

What to do

- Work with ten children and make sure that they know the counting rhyme, *Ten Fat Sausages*.

    'What do the sausages do when they are in the pan?'
    'Sometimes they go 'pop' and sometimes they go 'bang'.'

- Hand out the paper, and explain to the children that if they have a circle they write *pop* on it in big bold letters, but if they have a jagged shape like an explosion, they write *bang*.
- Explain to the children that they are all going to be sausages which explode in turn! When it is their turn, they will hold up their word and shout it out loudly before sitting down again.
- Now stand in a circle holding your papers, alternately pop and bang, and say the rhyme together.
- Don't forget to keep helping with the words of the rhyme, even after you have burst!

Tip This is a good opportunity to let the children work out for themselves how to spell the words.

Cross-curricular link

PSRN: Calculating.

What did you make?

Ask the children to make a label for their play dough model.

Aim

- To give the children a reason to write a simple caption.

Resources

- Dough, modelling tools
- Strips of stiff paper or card, folded so that they will stand like a place name

Preparation

- Lots of chances to use the dough in free play.
- Set up the dough table with a writing table next to it.
- Have a space ready to display the models and their labels.

What to do

- Over the day encourage children to make a model from the dough. They could choose a figure, an animal, a monster, etc. When their model is finished they should place it on the display.
- Now they go to the writing table and make a label. Show them how to make sure that they have the fold at the top so that their label will stand up.
- Decide which approach you want to take with the writing. This will depend on your children's abilities and experience:
  - Encourage the children to have a go with their own spelling as they write their label, e.g.

    Tom md a modl of a scry dinosor
    (Tom made a model of a scary dinosaur)

- Scribe the children's words for them as they watch you write.
- Prepare some sentences that the children can copy or adapt, e.g.

  . . . . *made a* . . . .
  . . . . *'s model is a* . . . .
  Here is a . . . .

- Talk about these with the children and read them together before they write.
- The children then stand the labels next to their models.

Vocabulary

push, pull, squeeze, made

Tip Try making the dough in a variety of colours by adding food colouring to the water before you mix it.

Cross-curricular link

PD: Using Equipment and Materials.

Cleaning your teeth

Create a special word bank with children who are beginning to write independently.

Aim

- To build a resource to support the children's writing.

Resources

- Small pieces of card
- An empty set of pockets labelled with the letters of the alphabet

Preparation

- Fix the empty word pockets near the writing table and sit near it with the children.

What to do

- Talk with the children about how they look after their teeth, before asking them to write about it.
- Ask the children if they can think of any words that they might use for today's writing, e.g.

  toothbrush, dentist

- Write the word boldly on a piece of card.
  – What sound does it start with?
  Sound it out as you write, at a level that these children will understand.
- Now, show the children the word. Read it together and identify the initial letter. The child who suggested the word can come out and place it in the pocket showing that letter. The others can help if necessary.

- Continue like this until you have a good supply of words on your topic.
- Ask any child to come out, choose a word from one of the pockets and read it out loud.
  - Does everyone agree?
- The child replaces it in the correct pocket.
  - Can the child remember where it goes?
- The children can now use this resource to help them with today's writing. Remind them where they can find the other key words.

  'These are just the special words for today'.

Vocabulary

toothbrush, toothpaste, dentist, rinse, no sweets, water

Tip Remove the cards at the end of the session so that your pockets are empty, ready for next time, or for the next group of children, who will have their own ideas.

Cross-curricular link

PD: Health and Bodily Awareness.

Welcome!

Help the children make cards for the new children joining your setting.

Aim

- To introduce children to the use of lists whilst writing with a purpose.

Resources

- A list of first names of the children about to join your setting
- Access to a computer and writing program

What to do

- Explain to the children that new children will soon be joining you, and they will be coming on a visit.
- Show them the list of names and read it to the children. Ask them to look at it carefully and notice how it is laid out.
- Tell them that you want them to design a welcome card for each person on this list.
  The children can work with you at the computer to choose and download a picture from a picture library.
- Then they can help you to create a message, e.g.

  Dear . . . . We are looking forward to playing with you here on Wednesday at 10 o'clock. Love from . . . . . .

- Leave a gap for the names of the recipients and the senders, as you will be adding these later. (If you prefer not to use the names of your current children at the end of the message use the name of the group, class or setting instead.)
- Encourage the children to choose the font, colour, layout, etc. within the boundaries you will give them. Then print out the cards.

- Each child in the group can now choose one name from the list to insert in a card and write their own name at the end.
- Remind the children to tick the name they have chosen off the list so that no one is missed out. Talk about the list being a useful way to make sure of this.
- Read through the cards again with the children, checking against the list to make sure that everyone has got a card.

Tip **You may need to write some of your cards in a home language other than English.**

Cross-curricular link

PSED: Making Relationships.

Answer the question

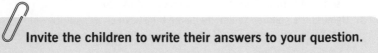

Invite the children to write their answers to your question.

Aim

- To provide an opportunity for children to write independently.

Resources

- An attractive box in which to collect answers
- Paper and pencils

Preparation

- Choose an open question to ask the children, e.g.

  'What do you like doing best at school?'

- Print out or write your question in large font.

What to do

- Show the children the question, and ask them if anyone can read it. Encourage them to try, and then read the question to the children, pointing at each word as you do so.
- Explain to the children that you're interested in their answers but you haven't time to listen to everyone now.

  'Please can you write your answers down and put them in the box for me to read later?'

- Show the children the box for their answers.
- Pin the question on the wall near the box.
- Remind the children to put their names on, otherwise you won't know who likes what.

- Later in the day open the box with the children and read their replies. Praise the children's attempts.
- Next time choose a different question to ask, e.g.

  'Who did you play with today?'

Vocabulary

question, answer, what, who, when, where, how

Tip This is a good opportunity to assess the children's use of their phonic knowledge in their writing.

Cross-curricular link

PSED: Sense of Community.

Hoop·la

A game for composing sentences on the go. The children jump from hoop to hoop to choose their words.

Aim

- To help children to form simple sentences.

Resources

- Five hoops
- Large pieces of card

Preparation

- Write one key word on each piece of card, e.g.

    Tom   can   see   a   dog

- Lay out the hoops in a circle.
- Place one of your cards in each hoop.

What to do

- Explain to the children that they are going to make some sentences from the words in the hoops. Spend some time reading each word.
- Demonstrate the activity yourself by reading all the words again out loud, and then talking through the process of choosing your sentence. From these five words you could make,

    Tom can see a dog
    a dog can see Tom
    can Tom see a dog
    can a dog see Tom

- Now, step into the hoop that has your first word in it, and say it out loud. Look for your second word, jump into that hoop and say it out loud. Continue through your sentence.
- Choose a child to have a go. Help the child to plan a sentence from the available words, and then jump into the hoops, saying the words out loud at the same time.
  Each child in turn can now have a go.

  'Which sentence will you make?'

- Encourage the other children to watch and listen carefully.

Vocabulary

sentence

Tip Increase the choice of words for more able children or add punctuation cards and capital letters for some words.

Cross-curricular link

PD: Movement and Space.

Letters in the sand

Hide letters in the sand and watch as the children have fun making CVC words.

Aim

- To encourage children to use their knowledge of phoneme/grapheme correspondence to spell simple words.

Resources

- Three plastic washing up bowls in different colours, filled with sand
- Magnetic letters
- Individual magnetic boards

Preparation

- Place the letters in the sand in the three bowls:
- Two bowls will each have the same set of consonants, e.g.

    s, t, p, n, c, d, g, h, m, r

- One bowl will have several of each of the five vowels.
- From these you can make at least:

    can, cat, cut, dog, dig, man, mat, sit, sat, set, met, net, pan, pin, pen, pot, pit, sun, ran, run, rat, hat, hot, hen

What to do

- Sit in a circle with the children, with the bowls in the middle.
- Choose one child to come out and pick one letter from each bowl in turn. Identify the letters as they are chosen, and place them on a magnetic board. Show the children how you can arrange them to make a simple word. Read it together by segmenting and then blending the letter sounds.

- Children can now work in pairs to choose one letter from each bowl (unseen) and make another word with them on their board.
  - Can you read it?
  - Is it a real word?
- When everyone has made a word ask the children to hold up their boards so that everyone can see their word. Go round the circle reading the words together.
  - Can anyone make a different word with the same letters?

Vocabulary

consonant, vowel, sound, letter, word

Tip Leave the bowls out near a large magnetic board. Collect as many words as you can. Read them together at the end of the session.

Cross-curricular link

CLL: Reading a Range of Simple Words.

Gordon's garage (2)

> Use your old and damaged toy cars to produce a price list of repairs with the children.

Aim

- To encourage the children to use reading and writing in their role play.

Resources

- Broken or damaged toy vehicles
- Large sheet of card and pens

Preparation

- Write *Gordon's Price List* at the top of the piece of card.
- Mark the card with faint lines for guiding the writing.

What to do

- Sit round a table with a box of well-used or damaged toy vehicles.
- Let the children examine them for damage. Talk about what is wrong with them.
- Explain to the children that they are going to decide how much Gordon will charge for repairing the vehicles. Ask one child to describe what is wrong with the vehicle he has picked out, e.g.

    It needs a new tyre.

- Ask the group what Gordon should charge for putting on a new tyre. Work in pounds, using numbers that your children can handle. Agree on a figure, e.g.

    £10

- Show the children the large piece of card and read the words at the top: *Gordon's Price List*.

- Use a piece of paper to work out with the children how to write down, e.g.

  1 new tyre £10

  One child can now copy this onto the price list with a bold-coloured pen.
- Continue around the group, describing the damage to a vehicle, working out the price and writing it down on the price list.

Vocabulary

damage, repair, price. Vehicle parts: tyre, windscreen, headlights, etc.

Tip This writing activity should appeal to boys.

Cross-curricular link

PSRN: Numbers as Labels and for Counting.

Who was kind today?

Write a question that invites children to notice and record positive behaviour in the setting.

Aim

- To provide an opportunity for children to read and write familiar words.

Resources

- A whiteboard and pens

Preparation

- Write the question at the top of the whiteboard, e.g.

  Who was kind today?

What to do

- Show the children the board and read the question together. Explain to them that today they should be looking out for anyone that they notice being kind to someone else.
- If they see someone being kind they should write that person's name on the board, e.g.

  If you see Jamie helping Sam to pick up the pencils that he knocked over – without anyone asking him to do it – then Jamie is being kind. You can write Jamie's name on the whiteboard.

- Encourage the children to suggest other kind things that they might see.
- At the end of the day, sit in a circle with the children. Look at the whiteboard and count up all the names.
- Ask who wrote a name on the board. In turn, the children can come out and tell everyone what they saw, and why they thought it was kind. Everyone can clap them for noticing.
- All the children whose names are on the list then stand up and everyone gives them a clap.

Vocabulary

kind, friendly, helpful, polite

 Tip Next time you use this activity, change the word at the top of the whiteboard. Try 'hard-working' or 'busy' instead.

Cross-curricular link

PSED: Making Relationships.

Lucky dip

Play a simple game of lucky dip to give your children a fun reason to write their name.

Aim

- To support the children in recognising and writing their own names.

Resources

- Small scraps of paper and pencils
- A recycled plastic ice-cream tub or a drawstring bag to hold all the names

What to do

- Explain to the children that you are going to play lucky dip.

    'Does anyone know what the game is?'

- Explain that everyone's name – written on a piece of paper – is going into this tub or bag, then someone will close their eyes and take out one of the papers.
  They will open the paper and read the name.

    'If it's your name then you are the winner!'

- Help the children to write their names on small pieces of paper. Remind them to write their name clearly so that another person can read it. Then show them how to fold their paper and then drop it into the tub or bag.
- When everyone's name is in, give the bag or tub a good shake.

    'Does anyone know why I'm shaking the bag?'

  Do the children understand why this is a fair way to choose a name?
- Now for the exciting part . . . Ask another adult to close their eyes and put their hand into the bag and choose a paper. Unfold the paper carefully and read the name. Give them a clap!

- That child can be the first one to get their coat or snack or go to lunch. But before they go, they must close their eyes and reach into the bag and choose a paper. They can then unfold the paper.

   'Can you read the name?'

   Carry on for three or four names.
- Leave the bag around so that the children can carry on playing if they wish.

Vocabulary

lucky dip, name, fold, unfold, first, second, third, fourth

Tip Remember to discard the names that have been chosen so they are not picked out again.

Cross-curricular link

PSED: Making Relationships.

Make a board game (1)

Help the children make a simple board game starting with wrapping paper.

Aim

- To provide a purpose for children to write captions.

Resources

- A piece of colourful wrapping paper (cut to fit the size of your laminator)
- Twenty small squares of paper for the track – 15 in one colour and five in a different colour
- Pens, paper and glue

Preparation

- Lots of opportunities for the children to play board games.

What to do

- Work with a small group of children around a table.
  Explain to them that you are going to make your own board game to play.
- Lay out the wrapping paper and show them how the track will be made with the small squares.
  - Do they understand why there need to be some different coloured squares?
- Help the children write one number on each square. Then stick the track onto the wrapping paper.
- Help the children write 'start' and 'finish' in the appropriate places.
- You might decide to think of a title for the game together and scribe it for them on the wrapping paper in bold print.

- Now plan with the children what captions to write next to the five differently coloured squares, e.g.

    miss a turn/go back one square/have another go/go on one square

- Help the children to write the captions carefully so that others can read them and glue them near the coloured squares. If possible, laminate the game to make it more durable.
- Play the game with counters and dice.

Vocabulary

Instructions – e.g. miss a turn/go back one square/have another go/go on one square

Tip Adapt the activity to suit the ability of your children, e.g. for the youngest children you can have the numbers already written so the children can place them in the correct order and you can scribe their ideas for captions.

Cross-curricular link

PSRN: Numbers as Labels and for Counting.

Make a board game (2)

> Make a board game with the children using their own drawings for the board.

Aim

- To make and play a game involving the children in recognising letter sounds.

Resources

- A3 card
- Twenty small squares of paper – you will need ten in one colour and ten in another
- A set of letters on cards
- Felt pens and glue

Preparation

- Select the letter sounds you want the children to practise.

What to do

- Work with a small group of children around a table. Explain that you are going to make a board game that involves recognising letter sounds.
- Choose a title for the game, e.g. 'What sound?' and write it on the card in bold print.
- Ask them to draw pictures on the A3 piece of card. Use ideas from a story or the theme you are working on, e.g. mini-beasts.
- Show them how the track will be made with the small squares.
- Help the children arrange the squares in a pattern along the track, e.g. alternate the colours, or place two of one colour then two of the other.

- Help the children write one number on each square and then stick the track onto the decorated card. Help the children write 'start' and 'finish' in the appropriate places.
- Ask the children to choose one of the colours. Explain to the children that whenever they land on this colour they have to pick up a card. Show the children the letter cards and tell them they must say the sound for this letter. Then they return the card to the bottom of the pile.
- Tell the children if they get the letter sound wrong they stay on the same square, but if they get it right they move on to the next square. Let everyone take a letter card in turn to check that they understand.
- Then play the game using counters and dice.
- The winner is the first to get to the finish.

Vocabulary

numbers 1–20, letter sounds

Tip   You could also use this game with key word cards.

Cross-curricular link

PSED: Making Relationships.

Chapter 9
Making a book

Garden centre (3)

Introduce the children to this counting poem and add number words to their pictures to create your own version.

Aim

- To write a poem with the children.

Resources

- 'Garden Rhyme' p. 125 in Toczek, N. and Cookson, P. (2007) *Read Me Out Loud. A Poem to Rap, Chant, Whisper or Shout for Every Day of the Year*, London: Macmillan Children's Books
- Ten sheets of mounting paper
- Painting materials

Preparation

- Children can create some paintings of garden-related items.
- Cut them out and mount them in groups so that you have, e.g. one greenhouse, two wheelbarrows, three spades and so on up to ten.
- Use any spare pictures to create a cover, with the title *A Counting Poem*.

What to do

- Read the poem 'Garden Rhyme' to the children.
- Ask them to spot the patterns: every line starts with a number, and the numbers are in order. Practise your counting.
- Some of the lines rhyme. Can the children guess what the rhyming word will be if you pause just before it?
- Read it several times to let the children become familiar with it.
- Now bring out your paintings.
  - Can the children find a paper with just one item on it?
  - You write the label for it, e.g. *One greenhouse*.

- – Can they find the paper with two items on it?
- – You scribe again, e.g. 'Two wheelbarrows'.
  Continue in this way up to ten items on any page.
- Now you can all read your class version of the poem.
- This would be a useful format for any theme that you are focusing on.

Vocabulary

number words, rhyme

Tip Staple the pages together inside the cover to make a counting book.

Cross-curricular link

PSRN: Numbers as Labels and for Counting.

Garden centre (4)

Make a large concertina-style book with the children to demonstrate the lifecycle of a plant.

Aim

- To involve children in organising writing.

Resources

- Six sheets of strong A4 paper
- The set of six plant stages models made in: Garden centre (1) (see p. 8).

Preparation

- Make the book by fixing six sheets of strong paper at the sides to form a concertina.

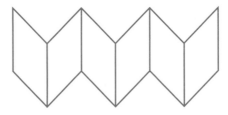

- Show the children the models they made of plants in varying stages of growth. As you do this, engage the children in discussions on the changes that are occurring as the plants grow.

What to do

- Encourage the children to order the six pots in their stages of growth. Stress the importance of the left to right ordering, as this will match their writing.
- Ask the children:

    'Where is the seed in the first pot?'
    'In the soil.'

    Scribe the words *'The seed is in the soil'* on the first page of the concertina book.
- Ask the children how they know when the seed is starting to grow.
    'It has a shoot.'
    Write *'It has a shoot'* on the second page.
- Continue like this until you have:

    It is in the soil
    It has a shoot
    It has a leaf
    It has a bud
    It has a flower
    The flower has seeds.

- Show the children how you can now stick the last page to the first page and have a complete cycle of events – a lifecycle.

Vocabulary

seed, shoot, leaves, bud, soil, flowers

Tip Leave out some small concertina-folded 'books' on the writing table for the children to make their own versions if they wish.

Cross-curricular link

KUW: Exploration and Investigation.

Big book, little book

Make some books for the Three Bears and encourage the children to match their writing to the size of the book.

Aim

- To provide an opportunity for children to use writing in their play.

Resources

- Paper, card
- Pens, pencils and crayons

Preparation

- Make some books with brightly coloured covers by stapling folded sheets of paper into a card cover. Make them in three different sizes.
- Write and draw the same information in one of each size, e.g. 'This is my bed.' 'This is my bowl.' 'This is my chair.' Match the drawing and writing to the size of the book.

What to do

- Show the children three of the books you have created. Discuss with the children:
  - What do they notice about them?
  - Can they identify them as big, medium and small?
  - Which family might own these books?
- Now look inside the books. Encourage the children to notice that they all have the same writing and pictures in them.
- Describe the writing – is it small, or bigger, or in-between-sized? Encourage as many descriptions of the size, or the comparisons between the sizes, as the children can suggest.

- Tell the children that they will find sets of books like this on the writing table, if they would like to make some more books for the bear family.
- Remind the children to match the size of their writing and drawing to the size of the book they have chosen.

Vocabulary

big, large, medium, in-between, small, little

Tip Prepare a 'bookcase' for the bears in your role-play cottage and encourage the children to read the books when they are playing in there.

Cross-curricular link

PSRN: Shape, Space and Measures.

My house

> The children sing a song and write a book about the number of people who live in their house.

Aim

- To help children use writing as a means of recording.

Resources

- 'How many people live in your house?' in *Tinder-box: 66 Songs for Children* (1983) London: A & C Black
- Three sheets of A4 paper and one piece of A4 card per book, enough for one book per child.

Preparation

- To make each book:
  - Lay three pieces of paper on the piece of card.
  - Fold the card and paper down the centre and staple together.
  - Then cut off the two top corners to create a roof shape.
  - Write on the last page . . . . *live in my house.*
- Make an extra book for yourself for demonstrating.

What to do

- Sing the song – *How many people live in your house?*

  Talk with the children about who lives in their house.
  Tell them they're going to make a book about how many people and animals live in their house.

- Show the children your book. Demonstrate:

  How to decorate the front and back with doors and windows.
  How each person or animal is drawn on a new page.

When you have completed the pictures in this book about your house, count them up and complete your final sentence.

- Encourage the children to draw and write in their book. Help the children complete the final sentence by counting and then writing the number in their house.
- The children can read their books to themselves, their friends, other adults, parents and carers.

Vocabulary

mum, dad, sister, brother, baby, dog, cat, rabbit, guinea pig . . .

Tip Remember to be sensitive about children with absent parents etc. Focusing on the number in their house and including animals can be helpful for this.

Cross-curricular link

PSRN: Numbers as Labels and for Counting.

Five Little Ducks

Help the children make their own individual book of the rhyme.

Aim

- To encourage children's familiarity with how books work.

Resources

- A4 paper and card.

Preparation

- Make books for the children:
  - A piece of card folded in half with two pieces of paper the same size stapled inside.
  - Write *Five Little Ducks* as the title on the front of each book.
- Make sure everyone knows the rhyme.

What to do

- Give everyone a book and tell them they are going to make a book about the rhyme.
  Can they all find the front?
- Encourage the children to open the book and draw a pond on the first page. Ask how many ducks are on the pond at the start of the poem. Help them draw five ducks on the pond.
- Then everyone turns over to the next page and draws another pond. Ask how many ducks came back this time. Help the children draw four ducks on this pond.
- Continue through the book showing 5, 4, 3, 2, 1, 0 ducks. Make the final page the same as the first when the five little ducks come swimming back.
- More able children might enjoy writing the numbers on each page.
- Write the children's names on the back cover and leave the books available for other children to read.

Vocabulary

five, four, three, two, one, none, front cover, title, author, page, turn over, next, back cover

Tip   Be careful that children don't turn over two pages at once!

Cross-curricular link

PSRN: Calculating.

Going for a walk

After a walk with the children, make a class book based on *Rosie's Walk* by Pat Hutchins. The children can then make cardboard figures that take a walk through the book.

Aim

- To make a book about an activity the children have done.

Resources

- A3 pieces of paper
- Two A3 pieces of card for the cover
- Small pieces of card
- A copy of Hutchins, P. (2001) *Rosie's Walk*, London: Red Fox Books

Preparation

- Take the children for a walk around their local area.
- Talk about places you pass as you walk.

What to do

- When you get back, talk about your walk and read the children *Rosie's Walk*. Tell the children they are going to make a book about their walk.
- Make a list of the places in the order that you walked, using prepositions, e.g.
  - out of the gate
  - down the hill
  - across the road
  - past the shops
  - around the park

- Let the children choose which part of the walk they draw. Then an adult can scribe the appropriate descriptive phrase below their picture.
- The pages are stapled together with a front and back cover to form a book. Write *Our Walk* as the title, and encourage everyone to read it.
- Each child now draws a picture of themselves on a small piece of card. Then they can take turns to read the book and 'walk' their cardboard figure across each page.

Vocabulary

through, around, past, across, down, under

Tip The cardboard figures can be kept in pockets made on the inside of the back cover.

Cross-curricular link

KUW: Place.

'What is White?' by Mary O'Neil

Use this poem as an inspiration to write your own colour poem with the children.

Aim

- To write a poem with the children, scribing for them.

Resources

- Mary O'Neil's poem 'What is White?' can be found in Rumble, A. (1989) *Is a Caterpillar Ticklish?,* London: Puffin Books

Preparation

- This poem lists things that are white. There are lots of interesting words to discuss as you enjoy it together.
- If your children are very young it may be better to use only one section of the poem.

What to do

- Tell the children you are going to write a new poem about a colour. Choose a colour together for your title, e.g.

    What is red?

- Collect ideas of things that colour, e.g. traffic lights (see vocabulary list below for more ideas). Scribe the children's ideas.
- Then help them to extend them into descriptive phrases, e.g.

    Red means stop

- Develop the children's phrases, e.g.

    A glowing red light warning us of danger

- Prompt the children to use all five senses when describing and extending their ideas.
- Then, write the phrases in a list to create a simple poem, e.g.

  What is red?
  A glowing red light warning us of danger
  Red poppies growing in a field
  Paper poppies to wear with a pin
  A huge red fire engine screeching by.

Vocabulary

fire engine, poppies, postboxes, blushing cheeks, fire, traffic lights, danger, sunset, blood, hearts, roses, apples, lipstick, clowns' noses

Tip The children can illustrate each line of their poem to create a poetry book.

Cross-curricular link

KUW: Place.

Our day

Take photographs with the children to keep a record of your daily routine and fix these into a book to tell the story of 'Our Day'.

Aim

- To make a book about the activities the children have been doing.

Resources

- Camera
- A large scrapbook

Preparation

- Help the children take photographs of each other at significant times throughout the day, e.g. hanging up their coat as they arrive, story time, play time, lunch time.

What to do

- Look at the photographs together. Encourage the children to explain what's happening in each photograph. Decide which photograph shows the beginning of the day.
- Then put them in order showing the routines of the day. Ask:

  'What comes next?'
  'Do we do this before or after that?'
  'What happens after that?'
  'How does our day end?'

- Let the children fix the photographs into the book in the correct sequence.
  Read the book to them using story language and time connectives, e.g. first, later, in the end.
- Encourage them to take turns to tell the story of our day.

Vocabulary

first, then, next, after that, later, in the end

 Tip For older children the adult could scribe the story to accompany each photograph.

Cross-curricular link

PSRN: Shape, Space and Measures.

In my lunch box

Help the children make their own simple lift-the-flap book based on lunch-box meals.

Aim

- To develop children's awareness of the way stories are structured.

Resources

- Books about food
- A lift-the-flap book
- A4 paper and card to make individual books
- Small pieces of paper and sticky tape

Preparation

- Make a lunch-box-shaped book:
  - Lay three sheets of paper between two sheets of card and staple the long lower edge so that the 'book' opens at the top like a lunch box.
- On the first page write, *In my lunch box I have . . .*

What to do

- Show the children a lift-the-flap book and examine how it works.
- Show them the lunch-box books you have prepared, and the smaller pieces of paper. Demonstrate how to stick a piece of paper on so that it can be lifted up, just like the flaps in the book.
- Read the words you have written on the first page of the lunch-box book. Encourage the children to suggest some things that might be in a lunch box.
  Look at your food books and a picture dictionary together for other ideas.

- The children can now draw one picture on each page of something from their lunch box. Then, help them to write the names of these foods on small pieces of paper.

   Remember to put only one word on a piece of paper!

- Help them attach these as flaps to hide their drawings.

   'Can you read your own book?'
   'Can you read your friend's book?'

Vocabulary

Any food items chosen by the children

Tip Using sticky tape that is ready cut will make the children more independent when attaching their flaps.

Cross-curricular link

PD: Health and Bodily Awareness.

Do you know your ABC?

The children will enjoy choosing what to draw in their tiny alphabet books.

Aim

- To provide an opportunity for children to use word banks and other resources.

Resources

- Picture dictionaries
- Classroom word banks
- A4 paper

Preparation

- Cut the A4 paper in half, then fold seven of these sheets in half and staple them together to make tiny books.
- Print out the title '*Alphabet book*' – one copy for each book.
- Make sure the children know an alphabet song or have some understanding of the alphabet before doing this activity.

What to do

- Work with a small group of children.
  Let the children work in pairs with a picture dictionary.
  Ask them to look for something beginning with 'a'.
  Remind the children that this is the name of the letter.

  'What can you find that begins with the letter "a"?'

- Encourage the children to negotiate between themselves so that the books aren't identical.

  'Try to choose something different from your partner.'
  e.g. apple and alligator

- Show them the tiny books you have made. Ask them to stick the title 'Alphabet Book' on the front cover, then write their name underneath the title.
- Help them write the letter 'a' on the top corner of the first page of their book. Then they can draw their chosen item on that page.
- You might choose to do six letters at a time and complete the other pages over several sessions,
- Or you may decide to help the children write all 26 letters on individual pages first so the children can complete their books independently at the writing table when they choose.

Vocabulary

The names of the letters of the alphabet

Tip Use the opportunity to observe the children as they write their letters, and make a note of any letter formation problems.

Cross-curricular link

PSED: Making Relationships.

Joe's space journey

Encourage the children to imagine strange and wonderful things that Joe will discover on the planets that he visits.

Aim

- To enable children to create and use a word bank to write a story.

Resources

- A large sheet of black paper
- Sticky stars – gold and silver
- Paint
- Sticky labels
- Rocket-shaped books

Preparation

- Make some rocket-shaped books from paper and card.
- The children paint five or six brightly coloured planets on the black paper.
- Stick the stars all around them, and leave to dry.

What to do

- Work with a small group of children and help them to make up some names for the planets. These can be made-up words.
- Try to make words which the children will be able to spell at their own level of phonic knowledge, e.g. Zar, Bod, Lub, Niz.
- Encourage the children to write the name on a sticky label, and fix it near the chosen planet.
- Use a model space figure to be Joe and decide which planet he lives on.
  Tell the children,

  'Joe is going on a space adventure and we're going to tell his story.'

- Start from Joe's home and move him across space to another planet.
  Ask the children,

    'What will he see there?'
- Write their suggestions on sticky labels to attach near the planets, e.g.
  - blue trees
  - a dog that has green and yellow stripes

  Read the words together to remind everyone of what they say.
- Give the children a rocket-shaped book each to write their own version of Joe's journey, using the words on the picture as a word bank.

Vocabulary

Any words that the children want to use

Tip This is an activity for those children who can already write some of the key words.

Cross-curricular link

CLL: Story Settings.

Special days out

> Encourage the children to take home a doll when they have a special event at home. Help them record the visit in a class book.

Aim

- To inspire the children to record events in words and pictures.

Resources

- Two rag dolls or knitted dolls: one boy, one girl
- Paper, pencils etc., scissors and glue
- Sheets of sugar paper and some cord

Preparation

- To make the book:
  - Cut the sheets of sugar paper in half.
  - Punch holes in the left-hand side of the paper.
  - Tie the sheets together with the cord.
  - Put a photograph of your dolls on the cover of the book, and write '*Special days out with Tara and Toby*' (use your chosen names!) as the title.
- The children should already be familiar with the dolls and know their names. Encourage the children to take a doll home whenever they know they will be having a special day within their family, e.g. a birthday, a visit to Gran, a festival or family gathering such as Easter, Diwali or Eid, to link in with your work on festivals and other special occasions. Send home a notice about this for parents so that they understand what it is all about.

What to do

- The day after a child has taken one of the dolls home, sit together in a circle. The child who took the doll home stands next to you, holding the doll. They tell the others about the special things that Toby or Tara did, the place they visited, or about a special meal they shared.
- Encourage the children to ask questions so that the child with the doll can expand on the basic information. Try to include questions about the doll's 'feelings'. *'Was Tara excited about . . . . . .?' 'Was Toby pleased to see . . . . again?'*
- Later in the session spend time one-to-one with the child. Help the child to form one or two sentences to describe the doll's experiences and perhaps its 'feelings' during the visit. Scribe for the child or help the child to write the ideas down, according to their individual ability.
- The child can now stick their writing onto a page in the class book, and illustrate it.
- Share the book regularly with the whole group.

Tip If they have any photographs, tickets, invitations, programmes, etc., these could also be stuck in.

Cross-curricular link

KUW: Communities.

On Friday Something Funny Happened by John Prater

Enjoy the book with the children, then help them write their own additions to the text.

Aim

- To encourage children to use story language when they write.

Resources

- A copy of Prater, J. (1984) *On Friday Something Funny Happened*, London: Picture Puffins, or a different book that contains pictures without text
- Paper, pencils, reusable adhesive

Preparation

- Enjoy the book together.

What to do

- Working with a small group of children, look at the pictures of the children's adventures.
- Ask the children what's happening in the different parts of the story.
- Encourage the children to describe the children's activities as shown in the pictures.
- Help the children phrase their sentences into story language. For example, a child might say, 'They're getting all muddy.'
  The adult replies, 'Yes, so let's say *"They jumped in puddles and got very muddy"*.'
- Listen to the children's ideas then choose one sentence for each part of the story. Continue through the book until everyone has a sentence to contribute.
- Give the children a piece of paper to write their sentence on.

- Help the children write their sentences.
- Use reusable adhesive to stick their writing on the pictures.
- Read the book again, encouraging each child to reread the part of the story they have written.

Vocabulary

Words appropriate to your chosen book

Tip Choose whether it is more suitable to scribe for your children, offer them support with their writing, or encourage them to write the sentences independently.

Cross-curricular link

KUW: Time.

My own notebook

A simple way for the children to make their own notebooks using old greetings cards.

Aim

- To provide evidence of how children choose to record information or ideas.

Resources

- A4 paper
- Old greetings cards, without inner pieces of paper
- Container – a basket or attractive box

Preparation

- You may need to reduce the size of the card to remove words such as 'Happy Birthday'.
- Stick a piece of paper over any written message inside the card.
- Lay the open greetings card on top of four sheets of A4 paper.
- Trim the edges to match the size of the card.

What to do

- Explain to the children that they are going to make some notebooks. Show them how to open up the card and lay the sheets of paper on. Help them to use a long-armed stapler to fix these together at the centre fold.
- The child will then write their own name on the cover or inside the cover. You should add the date in small figures at the beginning of the notebook. Keep these in the special basket or box.
- Talk to the children about some of the ways that they can use their notebook. Tell them that it is for their own writing, not for work that

you have asked them to do. Can they suggest anything they might use it for? e.g.
- to write down something they did today
- to make a list
- when they are playing a game such as schools or detectives
- whenever they need to write something down
- When the notebook is complete add the finishing date at the end of the book.
- Leave materials available for children to make a new notebook if they fill this one fairly quickly.

Vocabulary

staple, stapler, personal, notebook

> **Tip** Use this to check the children's emergent writing. How often are they choosing to write? Is their spelling or handwriting developing? It is a useful way to monitor these skills.

Cross-curricular link

PD: Using Equipment and Materials.

Penguin Small by Mick Inkpen

Help the children make their own penguin-shaped version of this super book.

Aim

- To provide an opportunity for children to retell a familiar story in writing.

Resources

- A copy of Inkpen, M. (1994) *Penguin Small*, London: Hodder Children's Books
- One piece of A4 white card and two sheets of A4 white paper per book

Preparation

- Fold and staple two sheets of A4 paper inside a folded A4 card to make each book.
- Cut the book into a simple penguin shape.
- Enjoy the picture book *Penguin Small* with the children.

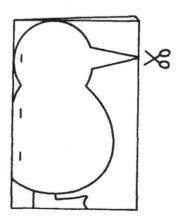

What to do

- Show the children the penguin-shaped books and talk about how to decorate the shape to make it look like *Penguin Small,* e.g. colour his back and head black.
- Help the children create their penguins by colouring his head, back and beak on the front and back cover.
- Explain that they are going to write the story of *Penguin Small*.
- Look at the first picture in the book and ask the children what's happening. Form a sentence together, e.g.

  'All the penguins swam away because the polar bears were nasty.'

- Help the children write the sentence on the first page in their book. Choose a method appropriate to the children: they may copy your writing, attempt it themselves or stick a printed version on the page.
- Now look at the second picture and ask why Penguin Small is sad.
- Continue in this way until you have summarised the story into eight sentences for the eight pages in their book.

Vocabulary

Past tense verbs – swam, met, floated, found, sailed, flapped, flew, spotted, soared

Tip Cover a display board with blue backing paper, then add large pieces of white card to the base line. You can then display the penguin books as if they are standing on icebergs.

Cross-curricular link

KUW: Place.

My Granny Went to Market by Stella Blackstone

Play games with the children to try to remember what Granny bought. Then they can make their own book recording some of the items.

Aim

- To provide materials and stimulus for children to create their own books.

Resources

- Blackstone, S. (2006) *My Granny Went to Market*, Bath: Barefoot Books
- A4 paper and A4 card
- Globe or map

Preparation

- Make individual books by stapling two sheets of paper into a folded piece of card.
- Read and enjoy the book *My Granny Went to Market* with the children.
- Type out copies of a title for the book and print it several times to fit the books you have made.

What to do

- After enjoying the book a few times, look on the map to find the countries mentioned.

   Ask the children what they know about each place.
   Maybe they come from that country, have visited there or have seen something about it in a book or on TV.

   Talk about the various items that Granny buys as she travels to different countries.

- Play a game with the children:
  - Open the book at a random place.
  - Tell the children the name of the country.
  - Ask what Granny bought there.
- Let the children take turns asking the questions.
- Play a traditional memory game:
  - Sit in a circle
  - Start the game by saying '*My Granny went to market and she bought a drum.*'
  - The next child says '*My Granny went to market and she bought a drum and a . . .*'.
  - The next child repeats the phrase and the two items and adds their idea.
  - Continue the game for as long as the children can remember the items in the list.
    (In the traditional game the items can be anything the children choose, but to play the game based on the book, list items mentioned in the book.)
- When the children have enjoyed playing these games a few times, show them the books you have prepared. Help them stick the title on the front of the book. Can they read it?
- Then let them draw pictures of all the items they can remember from the book. There are eight altogether. Can anyone remember them all?
- If appropriate, the children could copy labels for their pictures or you could act as a scribe.
- When they have finished their book, encourage them to write their name on the cover.
  Leave the books out for the children and their parents to enjoy.

Vocabulary

Japan, Australia, China, Mexico, Switzerland, Africa, Russia, Peru

Tip To extend this work about other countries provide books that show a range of languages, dress and customs from a variety of cultures.

Cross-curricular link

KUW: Communities.

Appendices

References

DfES references

DfES (2006) *Primary National Strategy. Primary Framework for Literacy and Mathematics*. Ref: 02011-2206
DfES (2007) *Letters and Sounds: Principles and Practice of High Quality Phonics*. Ref: 00282-2007.
DfES (2008) *Practice Guidance for the Early Years Foundation Stage. Non-statutory Guidance*. Ref: 00266-2008.

Useful websites

www.circle-time.co.uk
www.espresso.co.uk
www.zoes-world.co.uk

Artwork

A Bigger Splash by David Hockney
All Aboard by Zoe Kakolyris

Music

Soothing music e.g. Dvorak's *New World Symphony*
Strong, quick music e.g. Rimsky-Korsakov: *Flight of the Bumble Bee*
'How many people live in your house?' in *Tinder-box: 66 Songs for Children* (1983), London: A&C Black

Books

Ahlberg A. (1980) *Mrs Wobble the Waitress*, London: Puffin Books
Alakija, P. (2007) *Catch That Goat!: A Market Day in Nigeria*, Bath: Barefoot Books
Andreae, G. and Sharratt, N. (2002) *Pants*, London: Picture Corgi
Blackstone, S. (2006) *My Granny Went to Market*, Bath: Barefoot Books
Burningham, J. (1979) *Mr Gumpy's Motorcar,* London: Picture Puffins
Burningham, J. (1979) *Mr Gumpy's Outing*, London: Picture Puffins
Butterwick, N. (2008) *My Grandma is Wonderful*, London: Walker Books
Butterworth, N. and Inkpen, M. (2006) *Jasper's Beanstalk*, London: Hodder Children's Books

Carle, E. (2002) *The Very Hungry Caterpillar*, London: Puffin Books

Carle, E. (2009) *The Tiny Seed*, London: Simon & Schuster Children's

Collins, M. (2001) *Circle Time for the Very Young*, London: Paul Chapman Publishing

Exley, H. (2006) *Me and My Grandma*, Watford: Exley Publications

French, V. and Bartlett, A. (1995) *Oliver's Vegetables*, London: Hodder Children's

Garcia, E. (2009) *Toot Toot Beep Beep*, St Albans: Boxer Books

Hedderwick, M. (2010) *Katie Morag and the Two Grandmothers*, London: Red Fox Books

Holub, J. (2000) *Light the Candles: A Hannukah Lift-the-flap Book,* London: Picture Puffins

Hughes S. (1985) *Alfie Gives a Hand*, London: Collins Picture Lions

Hutchins, P. (1993) *The Surprise Party*, London: Red Fox Books

Hutchins, P. (2001) *Rosie's Walk*, London: Red Fox Books

Inkpen, M. (1994) *Penguin Small*, London: Hodder Children's Book

Mayo, M. (2003) *Emergency!*, London: Orchard Books

Prater, J. (1984) *On Friday Something Funny Happened*, London: Picture Puffins

Roennfeldt, R. (1980) *Tiddalick: The Frog Who Caused a Flood*, London: Picture Puffins

Rosen, M. (1993) *We're Going on a Bear Hunt*, London: Walker Books

Shoshan, B. (2005) *That's When I'm Happy*, London: Little Bee

Zucker, J. (2002) *Eight Candles to Light: A Chanukah Story*, London: Frances Lincoln

Zucker, J. (2005) *Lighting a Lamp: A Divali Story,* London: Frances Lincoln

Zucker, J. (2005) *Lanterns and Firecrackers: A Chinese New Year Story*, London: Frances Lincoln

Plus:

Your own choice of traditional tales

Sets of non-fiction books on a theme, e.g. mini-beasts, ducks, food

Poems and rhymes

'Fingers Like to Wiggle, Waggle' in Matterson, E. (compiler) (1991) *This Little Puffin*, London: Penguin

'Shop, Shop, Shopping' by Georgie Adams in Waters, F. (1999) *Time for a Rhyme*, London: Orion Children's Books

'Ten Dancing Dinosaurs' in Waters, F. (1999) *Time for a Rhyme*, London: Orion Children's Books

'Garden Rhyme' by Phil Rampton in Toczek, N. and Cookson, P. (2007) *Read Me Out Loud: A Poem to Rap, Chant, Whisper or Shout for Every Day of the Year*, London: Macmillan Children's Books

'What is White?' by Mary O'Neil in Rumble, A. (1989) *Is a Caterpillar Ticklish?*, London: Puffin Books

Number rhymes and action songs from:
Matterson, E. (compiler) (1991) *This Little Puffin*, London: Penguin
Good Morning Mrs Hen can be downloaded from **http://www.bigeyedowl.co.uk/show_songs.php?t=1**

Plus:
Your own choice of nursery rhymes.

Index of activities

Activity	Page number
Sense of Community	
Wedding (1)	16
Asking questions	36
Emergency! by Margaret Mayo (1)	14
Is it you?	62
Emergency! by Margaret Mayo (2)	72
After the big parade	76
Create a character	96
Candles (3)	116
Guess who! (1)	168
Guess who! (2)	170
Birthday (4)	242
What's in your box?	266
Wedding (2)	270
Answer the question	284

Problem-Solving, Reasoning and Numeracy

Numbers as Labels and for Counting	
Birthday (3)	154
Bags of words	160
Café (2)	186
Gordon's garage (2)	290
Make a board game (1)	296
Garden centre (3)	302
My house	308

Calculating	
Holidays (1)	122
Breakfast time	148
'Ten Dancing Dinosaurs' by John Foster	200
Good Morning Mrs Hen	214
Ten Fat Sausages	276
Five Little Ducks	310

Activity	Page number
Time	
My grandma	128
Holidays (2)	178
On Friday Something Funny Happened by John Prater	326
Place	
A Bigger Splash by David Hockney	92
Where are we?	152
Toot Toot Beep Beep by Emma Garcia (2)	190
Toot Toot Beep Beep by Emma Garcia (3)	192
Holidays (3)	272
Going for a walk	312
'What is white?' by Mary O'Neil	314
Penguin Small by Mick Inkpen	330
Communities	
Candles (1)	112
Catch that Goat! by Polly Alakija (1)	156
'Shop, Shop, Shopping' by Georgie Adams	196
Catch That Goat! by Polly Alakija (2)	202
Ribbon dance	238
Dear Bear	268
My Granny Went to Market by Stella Blackstone	332
Special days out	324

Physical Development

Movement and Space	
Follow-the-leader	10
Mini-beasts (2)	64
Candles (2)	114
Key word tunnels	172
Key word race	176
Hoop-la	286